Mindset for Success

Mindset for Success

Developing and maintaining the mindset to succeed in life & business

Reggie Batts

Acknowledgements
& Special Thanks

This book is dedicated to my parents, George Batts and Bobbie Batts. You have been model parents. I wish every child were blessed to have the amazing life experiences you both worked so hard to make sure I had. I honor you both! I can see you, Dad, smiling from heaven. I hope I've made you proud. To my amazing brothers and sister and their families (Tony, Tonee, Ewing, Lisa, Marvin), thank you for your constant and never-ending support.

JT Foxx, "the World's #1 Wealth Coach," thank you for your leadership and your selfless passion for helping others, including all you've done for me. You are the real deal!

Tony Robbins, thank you for first introducing me to this magnificent world of personal development & coaching. To the wonderful people in your organization who are still some of my dearest friends- I thank you all.

Thanks to all my family and friends worldwide. Special thanks to Damien Elston, who has been my coach for several years. There's no one in the business as good as you! My mentors who helped me throughout the years, Michael

Nitti, Gene McNaughton, John Assaraf, and so many more who have been awesome role models and have help mold me into the person I am today. Tony Luu, thanks for running everything in my business and being my left brain to manage it. You're a very talented singer & entrepreneur! Francie Baldwin, Joshua Trevino (Josh, you inspire me so much with your amazing story), Dallas Parrott (Dallas, you're a true leader), Peter Yonan, Danielle Itani (Danielle-the glue that held my Tony Robbins staff together), Les Evans, Stephan Fisher, Kevin France, Dana Van Hoose, Cherie Eilertsen, Les Evans, Dustin Roberts, Vikki Thomas, Brent Turley, Jason Evers, Jason Gilbert, Rose Chastain, and all my other friends, colleagues and clients all over the world: thank you for the contribution you've made in my life.

Table of Contents

What Is Success?

According to the *Business Dictionary*, success is the achievement of an action within a specified period of time or within a specified parameter. Success can also mean completing an objective or reaching a goal. Success can be expanded to encompass an entire project or be restricted to a single component of a project or task. It can be achieved within the workplace, or in an individual's personal life. For example, if an individual's personal goal is to be accepted in a new career, success would occur after the individual has been officially accepted into his or her new place of employment. Or to put it simply, it's a simple term used to describe a person that has achieved his or her personal, financial, or career goals.

Let's dive into it further:

Everyone thinks about success. In fact, a person will most likely spend his life trying to be successful. And coupled with that fact, we've all been programmed from our childhood to believe that achieving success starts with going to a good college. As we all know, the world is a competitive job market, and if one wants a high-paying job he needs some college credentials. Once one has graduated and has a well-paying job, he is on his way to becoming successful.

But success can be described in different ways because everyone has a different definition of success. For some, success is measured by social status and wealth, and for others, success is determined by the happiness one feels.

Which one is yours?

Earth, as we know it, is the planet where money is the value everyone seeks and wants and needs, making it the major concern for some people, unless you're Bill Gates or Donald Trump—the only problem this set of people have is the race to being recognized as the richest person on the planet.

To the point, money is a necessity for anyone who is trying to succeed in life. People work their whole lives trying to make money, so they can satisfy their desires. Don't you just love the idea of being able to point to something, say you want it, and get it? We all do. That's the dream.

Some state their views of success based on someone else's idea of what it is to be successful. But if we spend time and effort trying to meet somebody else's idea of success, and ignore or belittle our own views, then we'll end up being happy and exhausted. Some people define success as having their own home and having beautiful things in it. People take pride in what they own, either to show off that they're successful or not. Some people need to look successful in order to feel successful, which also basically meaning having nice things. It makes them feel good. And some, as mentioned above, define their success as happiness. These people find happiness in ways that don't necessarily have to involve money. Feeling loved is something that makes everyone happy, and that is a feeling of success. Many believe that life is not complete without love, which is why they struggle to be successful in this, and when they are, you can guess the feeling that comes with it. A person's work can also affect how happy he is. Some feel that it is more important to enjoy the work and get less money than it is to hate work and get paid more. Another factor in achieving psychological success is one's ability to enjoy what life gives him.

The most important realization an individual can make in his or her path to personal growth is to understand that there is no single formula that defines the path to personal success. We all have different goals and priorities—dreams—which means it's not the same activities that will make us feel good about ourselves. So, how is it that we can define success for each individual based on his or her natural strengths and weaknesses as well as inherited personality type?

Understanding what is important to you is "success"; so is recognizing your weaknesses and not hiding behind them. One cannot be successful until he has reached a certain mind-set of happiness. You can't be successful if you haven't reached a certain level of completing your goals and achievements.

But the only way to get that is by working hard and long. To be and feel successful, you need to have worked at it. A famous quote from Bob Brown goes like this: "Behind every successful man there are a lot of unsuccessful years." There are really no secrets to success. It is simply the result of preparation, hard work, and learning from one's failures that transition into success. Success takes a long time to get, it requires effort, but it is worth it eventually.

Sometimes, we feel success after a short-term goal, like completing that game or finishing a work project. What everyone doesn't get and still continues not to see is that a person's life is full of many little successes. It comes in any size.

But there is one big disadvantage to being fully successful. As the saying goes, "There are monsters under the bed." Success sometimes comes with a prize for some. Some people who are successful may be stressed, or have second thoughts about their life choices, or be unsure about the meaning of their life rather than the confident, popular, and consistently joyful people we see.

The media continues to give us what we want to see; so do the advertisers. They have successfully brainwashed us into accepting a facade; we have accepted the mask to be the real deal. This is a dangerous definition of success. We are shown people who are successful (and happy?), and they make us believe having lots of cash, living in a big house, owning all the latest things, from cars to technology to clothes, is the key to happiness and success. Stop being fooled by what you see; it is only a myth, a mirage. Achieving true success requires respect, appreciation, knowledge, wisdom, love, patience, and integrity, and because we're humans, these things can be difficult to attain. Living for nothing else but the pursuit of money and fame will not bring success and happiness for you. It might at first, but you grow tired of it. It is like a toy: a toy is fun when it's new, but after a few days or weeks, you grow tired of playing with it. One needs more than luxuries to live a fully successful life.

For example, having money won't help you have a successful relationship with your husband or wife—that can only be achieved through love and commitment, and then sacrifice.

"There is no elevator to success; you have to take the stairs."

When a person allows his mind to be restrained by the distractions of the world like the Internet or magazines or films, becoming successful becomes an impossible task. But it can be helped. We all know what happens with "impossible missions." Take a spin into Tom Cruise's *Mission: Impossible* films: those missions become possible in the end if the right amount of work and effort is put into them.

Ralph Waldo Emerson gave priceless insight when he wrote:

To laugh often and much;
To win the respect of intelligent people and the affection of children;
To earn the appreciation of honest critics and endure the betrayal of false friends;
To appreciate beauty;
To find the best in others;
To leave the world a bit better, whether by a healthy child, a garden patch or a redeemed social condition;
To know even one life has breathed easier because you have lived.
This is to have succeeded.

Emerson's quote provides a paradigm of success—a model to be admired and strived for. Emerson teaches that learning to appreciate what life has to offer makes it more enjoyable and interesting. And, yeah, doing something for others so they may benefit from you also brings happiness and satisfaction. Avoiding unnecessary conflicts, sparking lifelong friendships, learning patience, and developing leadership skills help one gain a better understanding of life, make well-informed decisions, and form healthy opinions, all of which are essential to becoming a successful person.

Bill Fitzpatrick, founder of the American Success Institute, said that a successful person is "strong when toughness is required and, at the same time, patient when understanding is needed." With this kind of thinking, you'll be setting yourself apart from mediocrity.

But, no doubt, being successful is a noble goal to strive for. It, however, requires practice. A lot of it.

Why Is Success Important?

Regardless of culture, race, religion, economic background, or social group, everyone agrees that success is important and vital to the well-being of the individual, the family unit, the group and, certainly, to the survival of those things in the future. Without continued success, the company, the dream, even entire races will cease to exist, as was the case with the Vikings, Romans, Greeks, American Indians, and then an endless list of companies and products. Success is important in that it is required in order to continue on.

Success isn't just important; it is vital and should never be reduced to anything less than vital. Success is valuable, important, and necessary for survival.

1. Success Leaves Footprints

In the world today, whatever you want to be successful in, there's a very good possibility that someone has already been successful in that field. It's like trying to create a brand-new superpower. You can't! Everything's been done. And successful people typically like to share their secrets. They have an innate desire to help people climb up the ladder, which is why some of them are invited to big conventions to give talks. Even if you have no one to teach you directly, simply following the footsteps of a successful person will put you halfway there.

Note, following a person's footsteps does not guarantee you success; it just "provides your actions with a scaffold to build upon." But remember, be creative about it. That's the only way you'll leave a different footprint and not be remembered as the duplicate of that successful person. You must define success on your terms.

2. Becoming Successful Is Not a Matter of Blind Luck or Chance

Success is a skill. And like other skills, it needs to be honed. It's a skill anyone can learn and grow in, either drastically or at a snail's pace. To be successful, you have to learn the art of success, by learning internal motivation and developing productive actions and powerful habits.

By learning and mastering the skill of becoming successful, you will be growing in confidence, you will be positively inspiring others to follow their dreams as well, and people will be attracted to you—interesting people who will find your work powerful and hopefully provide your life with richness as well as purpose, meaning, and direction. By mastering success, you gain control over your own life and are able to design a life rather than just live one (i.e., give your kids a better life).

3. String to the Past

Some of us don't realize it, but the things we do today are results of past events. Those memories successfully drive us to seek certain things and feel a certain way about things, like wanting to be the next Einstein or Michael Jackson. The past pushes us to want to be successful, as articulated in an example from an article I read on successsstory.com: "Tens of thousands of years ago, humans lived in small hunting groups and there were only two options—succeed (find food) or die. Fast forward to today; our brains still take success and failure as life or death and that is one major factor why it is so important to us as a species."

4. Success Stimulates

It pushes us to do better, be better at everything. It's what drives you to get out of bed in the morning and compels you to go out there, or better yet, makes you nuts when you're late for work. Knowing that there is a purpose, a goal we want to achieve, stimulates us to act. The more challenging the goal, the stronger success feeling is related to it. This way, we can get better motivation to achieve bigger goals, and we get additional stimulus to self-improve, grow personally, and learn to handle challenging goals. It also stimulates our brain so that we start to see things differently and reason better when a difficult situation arises and needs tackling. It pushes us to look at life differently, to see the value of living and, consequently, increase our sense of determination.

5. Success Inspires

The feeling of being inspired is indescribable. Success does that to one—chasing success does. And with inspiration comes mind opening. It drives one to think outside the box and understand more about what choices one should take and the path one should go. And success stories of others often inspire people to achieve something different. Having inspiration also molds one to become something better.

6. Family

The bond between the family is the strongest yet, which is why a husband would feel the urge to do everything within his power to make his wife and his kids have a better life, and a wife would do whatever she can to make her family stick together still. Success is all that. Family plays an essential part when it comes to success. Why? You want to be successful because of it.

7. Part of Our Life Plans

Everyone seeks success because it is part of the plan. It's basically everyone's dream, only everyone has a different dream in which to achieve it. We create milestones for ourselves, like goals to achieve and pursue. And achieving said milestones brings us positive feelings and emotions because we know that our life plans are fulfilling, and progress is being made.

8. Feelings to be experienced

We want to know how it feels. That is what success is to some of us. In our minds, we seek to know how it feels to be a pop star, singing on a stage; or how it feels to be an actor—to go on set, be someone else, be interviewed, be coworkers with other celebrities, be at comic conventions, and stand on a stage collecting Oscars. This little thing in our head drives us to want to be successful just like the kind of people we see on our screens, and some actually are successful at achieving just that.

9. Taste of Winning

Success pumps us up, makes our adrenaline rush, adds value to us, and inflates our egos. We love that feeling. It's a personal victory whenever we're more successful at something than another person is. Success can be seen as competition, a million people trying to achieve the same thing, and when one achieves that thing—that one feels like he's on top of the world.

10. Compensating for Our Past Mistakes

To err is human. Mistakes are inevitable. They're not nice or welcomed, but they are one of those things that always find you. Success pushes you to want to try what you have previously failed at and better it. It can also be viewed this way: success makes you want to avoid the errors of your father or mother. It's a force that pushes us toward goals that we have lost in, or lost our beliefs in, and forces us to attempt to beat it. The final victory at the moment you go through that thing that has been pulling you back compensates for all the previous failures and the sadness that came with them. It's kind of like a mother being in the pain of labor for over eight hours in the labor room and then birthing the baby. The eight hours of pain won't be remembered, just the joy. This pattern is very often a reason why we want to achieve success.

Personal Development

What is personal development? It is the pursuit of personal growth by attempting to expand self-awareness and knowledge and improve personal skills in order to realize and maximize one's full potential. The skills mentioned could be related to a person's mind or body.

The ultimate goal of personal development is to live one's life at a potential that brings one happiness. And to get there, to that level of self-accomplishment, there are some challenges, and unless you tackle these, personal growth is not really possible or at least not completely.

Personal development is a push—a struggle, you might say. A challenge. Nothing comes without the struggle and hustle. That's what life is all about. The struggle and the challenges make us. Sure, adapting to new things doesn't come easy, but that is what development is all about. Rome wasn't built in a day, you know. It might take time, and sometimes it might be that you have gone in one direction for far too long that simply going in another direction would be close to impossible. But nothing is impossible if you truly put your mind to it. And always remember, it is a lifelong process. If you're not going according to the pace you want, ironically, you're developing without knowing it.

As its name implies, personal development involves activities that improve awareness, identity, potential, skills, and talents. Personal development enhances an individual's quality of life and contributes largely to the realization and achievement of his goals and aspirations. There is no particular time frame as to how long a person can develop himself. Experts tell us that it happens over the course of a person's entire life.

Jim Rohn (famous author/speaker & one of my mentors) once said, "One day, my mentor, Mr. Earl Shoaff, said to me, 'Jim, if you want to be wealthy and happy, learn this lesson well: learn to work on yourself more than you do on a job.' I must admit that this is the most challenging assignment of all. This business of personal development lasts a lifetime."

Personal development is not limited to self-help. It entails the methods, principles, programs, tools, techniques, and assessment systems that support human development at a maximum individual level.

Before we totally delve into the way an individual can develop himself to his fullest potential, it is important to understand the concept known as self-awareness. According to Wikipedia, self-awareness is the capacity for intro-spection and the ability to recognize oneself as an individual separate from the environment and other individuals. The importance of self-awareness cannot be overemphasized. The moment you realize that you are a separate individual from the whole world, it becomes easy to realize that your success or failure depends primarily on you. It becomes easy to create a conviction of success, one that borders on helping yourself to achieve that.

To effectively manage your personal development, there are steps to take.

1. Develop your personal vision: Personal development could be for fun. Knowing where you want to be in a certain number of years is a great step in developing yourself. There should be a clear vision of where or what you want to be in a few months or years, and why you want to be in that place is a crucial part of developing your purpose.
2. Effective planning: Nothing has more effect than effective planning in any situation. Planning shows how you want to get to your vision, the activities you have put in place and the reasons why you want to be there at that particular time. You can also draw up a personal develop-ment plan. Even though it isn't necessary, it makes the planning process more realistic.

3. Record your personal development: It is usually a great idea to keep records of your personal improvement. You can begin by keeping a journal, which involves writing down your key developments in your learning process as they occur. This way, it becomes easy to reflect on your successes and mistakes at a later date. You then have the liberty to make improvements.

    This reflection makes it possible to motivate yourself and learn more skills in the future. Try to keep a learning log or journal as you develop your skills and knowledge.

4. Review and revise personal development plans: For effective learning, it is advised to reflect on your experiences. A popular dictum states experience is the best teacher. This is as true as ever. After reflection, careful consideration should be done to ascertain what you have learned from it and how to merge it into your personal development plans. This will also ensure that your activities move you toward your goal and that your vision and goal remain relevant to you.

Remember, Jim Rohn writes, "To have more than you've got, become more than you are."

There is the basic motivation to improve oneself. It either comes from inspiration or desperation. In other words, you either want to change because you watched something, or saw something, or heard something that's pushing you to be better than you already are, or you are looking to grow because of desperation, like something unpleasant happening that forces you to grow.

Basically, to grow, you have to keep learning, read books, learn new skills, and put yourself through things, but we'll talk about that more in one of the sections to follow.

This book is designed to help you think and teach you ways in which you can work toward goals, from how to be, to what to do—things that when read and understood thoroughly will help give you what you need so you can grow personally, enhance your employability prospects, raise your confidence, and lead to a more fulfilling, higher-quality life.

If you're still unclear and still find yourself thinking, "Why is personal development important?" the next question is for you.

Why Is Personal Development Important?

"There's only one corner of the universe you can be certain of improving, and that's your own self. So you have to begin there, not outside, not on other people. That comes afterwards when you've worked on your own corner."

—*ALDOUS HUXLEY*

1. Self-Awareness

The whole idea of personal development begins first with self-awareness. You truly find out who you are—that is, you learn about your values, your beliefs, the true purpose of your existence, your strengths and weaknesses, and your likes and dislikes. Observe your moods, reactions, and responses to what is happening around you. Become aware of how these moods and emotions affect your state of mind. Examine how you interact with others, and observe how your environment affects you.

We tend to underestimate the importance of knowing ourselves a lot. Many of us go through each day just reacting to events rather than making conscious choices based on who we are and what we want. When you don't know where you are headed, maybe you feel like there's a true purpose to your life, but you haven't discovered it yet. Deep down you wish you had this kind of knowledge that will push you forward. It's hard to set goals, get motivated, and determine the best course of action. But worry not, personal development cures all that; it helps you find your life's purpose.

There is no better feeling than chasing one's goals, and the pleasure gotten from the journey is vast. Self-awareness is the first and most important benefit of personal development.

First, dive into the deeper essences of who you are and find yourself; then design your life based on that person; and then chase your own goals and objectives.

Finally, knowing your life purpose will automatically shift you in different gears where you are empowered, inspired, and motivated to move forward in a given direction, with a mission and vision in mind. Personal development comes from simplifying one's life and listening to one's heart and intuition.

2. Sense of Direction

This is closely related to self-awareness. Have you ever sometimes sat down, pondered, and asked yourself where your life is heading, and most of the time, you get nothing? Well, with personal development you have a sense of direction, of where you want your life to head. Achieving self-awareness makes your sight clearer on the things you want from life. You can now live more productively. You can now let go of things that take a great deal of your time but are not important to your goal— your dream. It helps you to think about your ideal future, and motivate you to turn that vision of yours into reality. Always dream bigger! What is left for you now to do is keep track of your progress and celebrate your successes.

3. Improved Focus and Effectiveness

It's like being bathed in the Lazarus Pit. You go in dead, or very much ill, and come out more alive than ever. That's what personal development also gets you. No more blurry vision, only clarity. In this case, you might have a sense of direction now, but because you're still a living being, you'll find multiple tasks heading your way. But the more you grow, the more you know what your priorities are, like being able to pick out the task that will best give you the results you need with the resources available to you.

4. Motivation

With personal development, you can see clearly what the benefits of your actions are. Perhaps you don't like what you see ahead, but still, you'll be able to see if it is beneficial to you, which will allow you to decide yay or nay.

It helps you cultivate the right mind-set to endow yourself with enough energy and driving force to reach your goals. Self-motivation gets a lot of work done.

5. Resilience and Stress Management

As humans, we undoubtedly go through many things in life, some of them tough on us. Even having the right mind-set, you'll still feel the tough times in your life, but you'll be better equipped to deal with them. You will have been more confident, more resilient, and have personal and interpersonal skills to cope with anything that may come.

When you understand yourself better, you'll come to the realization that you're the only one responsible for your own life and that you're the only one who can control the reins of your life. That thought significantly reduces your stress. Why? Managing stress is all about taking charge of your thoughts, your emotions, your schedule, and the way you deal with your problems.

6. Relationships

Relationships can be a great thing and a devastating thing at the same time. Their effects on us are tremendous. They either lift us up or drastically drag us down. Developing personally will allow you to see which relationships are wasting your time and which are valuable.

Note, you have to develop the skills that will help you make the most of those relationships that have the most positive impact on your life. The better you understand yourself, the better you understand others, and the more your relationships will flourish. Creating a loving and accepting relationship with yourself first allows you to look deeper into what you believe about yourself.

7. Balance

A person's very cornerstone is a balanced lifestyle, including elements such as developing and maintaining good physical health and fitness, maintaining a good level of energy and vitality, having the ability to express your creativity, enjoying emotional and psychological stability, entertaining harmonious relationships, feeling and expressing your love toward people and life, acquiring effective stress management strategies and coping skills, and developing a sense of purpose and meaning in life.

8. Empowerment

In society today, people are not empowered to follow their natural selves. A lot of factors stop people from being who they really are, and some are for good reason, like education, societal norms, beliefs, values, governments, rules, ideologies have made many individuals stiff, not allowing them to move. It's like a disarming. People are made to believe they have no power over their fate. Granted, some of these factors are for a good cause, as there are psychopaths out there who'd ruin the world if given the opportunity. But a factor such as education can be helped: from childhood, children are programmed to be what the world wants them to be. Many times parents would dissuade their kids from developing personally, from following their own path. Instead they're egged on like horses being driven by a man, like a robot, with no space to actually find themselves.

One of the benefits of personal development is reclaiming your personal power—becoming empowered and remembering that you have all the inner resources you need to achieve all you want and develop to your highest potential.

9. Positive Attitudes

Knowing how to act—the kind of character to portray, the kind of personality, the kind of attitude—is something personal development brings you. Attitude is everything in life. Your attitude toward life makes all the difference between success and failure, fulfillment and losing oneself, empowerment and helplessness, happiness and deep anxiety.

Rather than feeling confused, helpless, anxious, and maybe cursed when something bad happens, have a positive mind-set and attitude toward said issue instead, and it will empower you.

10. Happiness

Happiness flows freely from its ocean if you know how to seek it. Everyone wants to be happy, and everyone deserves to be happy. There's simply no reason why you shouldn't live happily. You can find that ocean of happiness by relating better to life. The way we relate to life and give it meaning comes from a set of attitudes toward it.

A lot of personal development is having attitudes that will lead to our happiness. With that said, I believe our personal development is closely linked to happiness.

An article by Skillsyouneed.com shares a theory by a man named Abraham Maslow, and it is only right to share that with you. If I did not do so, I'd feel like I was making you miss out on a great thing, so here it is.

Abraham Maslow's Process Of Self-Actualization

A braham Maslow describes self-actualization as the desire that everybody has to become everything that they are capable of becoming. Put differently, it is self-fulfillment and the need to reach full one's potential as a unique human being.

Maslow (1970) suggests that all individuals have an inbuilt need for personal development which occurs through a process called self-actualisation.

The extent to which people are able to develop depends on certain needs being met and these needs form a hierarchy. Only when one level of need is satisfied can a higher one be developed. As change occurs throughout life, however, the level of need motivating someone's behavior at any one time will also change.

At the bottom of the hierarchy are the basic physiological needs for food, drink, sex and sleep, i.e., the basics for survival.

Second are the needs for safety and security in both the physical and economic sense.

Thirdly, progression can be made to satisfy the need for love and belonging.

The fourth level refers to meeting the need for self-esteem and self-worth. This is the level most closely related to self-empowerment.

The fifth level relates to the need to understand. This level includes more abstract ideas such as curiosity and the search for meaning or purpose and a deeper understanding.

The sixth relates to the aesthetic needs of beauty, symmetry and order.

Finally, at the top of Maslow's hierarchy is the need for self-actualisation. Maslow says that all individuals have the need to see themselves as competent and autonomous, also that every person has limitless room for growth.

To Abraham Maslow, the path to self-actualisation involves being in touch with your feelings, experiencing life fully and with total concentration.

Examples Of Personal Development Goals

According to EmployeeConnect, there are examples of goals you can infuse into your personal life. The following is a piece written by Byron Conway.

From the moment we have our first memory as a person, there is a need to learn. Personal growth starts during childhood, but it is consolidated during adolescence and youth.

At different stages of our lives, we find ourselves learning to do new things that will hopefully come in handy in the future. As I hinted before, the personal development of a person is the improvement in the person's conduct.

To develop oneself, there is an infinite number of things one can do. Note, developing yourself also makes the way people see you change for the better. Listed below are some achievable personal-development goals that will improve your life.

1. Learn a Language

You may find yourself wondering, how does learning a language make growth in my own self?

"Learning a language" doesn't necessarily have to mean learning a "new" language. We were all born into a certain language. That's basically what defines our nationality. As a kid, growing up, I wasn't that good at my mother tongue. I was good, but I was shaky, if you catch my drift.

As I began to progress in age, I started to realize—and also with the help of things around me like films, books, and even music—that I could be better, and I got better with that knowledge edging me on to keep learning the language, thereby growing.

My point: we never stop learning. You can learn a language by adding to the knowledge of what you already know.

But of course, you can learn a new language. Pick up on Spanish, French, German, or whatever.

In the world today, being multilingual can be an invaluable personal asset and help with your self-development. Although you can't become fluent in another language within a matter of months unless you're gifted with a super ability, knowing just a little bit of another language can be useful in certain situations and even provide opportunities for you. If, for example, in your workplace, there is a need to speak to a foreign person about an opportunity for the company, being multilingual could put you in the good graces of your boss or potential client.

2. Embracing Change

Change is one of those things everyone should constantly do. You can't expect to grow if you're stuck. Change is constant, and sometimes, attempts to resist change can be futile or might end up dragging you behind. Embracing change however it comes allows you to be in a better position to adapt to the new environment and make use of the opportunities it presents.

3. Responsibility

Taking responsibility for your actions is a clear example of personal development. When a person assumes responsibility, among the many things it shows is shows maturity—that is, growth.

Becoming responsible is something we should do, although it eludes some of us or has eluded some of us at some point in our life. Take children, for example: we can't expect children to be responsible for their age—although some of them show great responsibility even at a young age. But we can expect them to start becoming responsible after their youth. And in many cases, some people only learn to start becoming responsible when they leave their cocoon, their parents' house. And some become responsible when they're holding their two-minute-old babies in their hands, still all weak from the magic of childbirth or being in the room of childbirth, and staring into the eyes of their creation. That is when it hits them that they have to grow.

So, ask yourself, "Am I responsible?"

4. Behavior

Having and projecting the right behavior lifts you up the ladder. When you control your natural impulses and behavior in front of others, that is self-development.

In life, we will face a lot of situations that will put us down or cheer us up. During the situations that put us down, we should be tolerant of other people's opinions. Listening to other people's opinions and reacting accordingly and politely shows you are a person who has an improved behavior.

5. Self-Esteem

Self-development also implies that you must love yourself, no matter what. People worry about a number of things: teenagers worry about their looks and appearance, and they try to have that perfect body type, thereby hurting themselves in the process. You grow when you start accepting yourself the way you are and see yourself as something more than ordinary—something special.

With that said, it doesn't mean you have to forget about your appearance; it means you must understand that your look is just a part of you, and there are more valuable things inside you.

6. Confidence

Confidence! There will be moments when we'll have doubts and not know what to do. Self-development is knowing the decision you make might work out or not work out, but you still make it anyway. Being sure about oneself and having the ability to face the obstacles that may arise.

> In a study conducted in 1921 by Dr. Lewis Terman of Stanford University involving over 1,500 gifted children, the study revealed that IQ is not the most important ingredient for success. Instead, Terman found that there were three factors that were much more important than intelligence in determining success. One of these is self-confidence (the other two were setting goals and persevering).
>
> Your self-esteem, or your self-confidence, is basically what you think about yourself: how competent you think you are in dealing with life's challenges, and how worthy you feel of happiness and success. One of the reasons why bolstering your self-confidence is important is because there's a strong correlation between confidence and success.
>
> Therefore, one of your self-development goals should be to increase your self-confidence.

7. Know Your Klout Score

The "Klout" website helps you in finding out what you can do to improve your life, as it pertains to your social media.

Simply sign up to Klout and connect your social media accounts—and then investigate what you can do to improve them.

8. Constructive Arguing

Yes, it could be said that arguments are bad, but for the most part, they are unavoidable. Things happen. But instead of ranting on during an argument, approaching them in the right way is growth.

The key is to learn how to argue constructively, which often means keeping emotions in check and showing greater consideration for the views of others. Having the ability to resolve disagreements rationally and settle disputes amicably will make you happier and more successful.

9. Time Management

When you don't have a clear plan of what your next steps are, it's easy to waste time. But employing time-management techniques can help you improve your punctuality and professionalism while making more time for the things that are really important to you.

10. Creativity

Everyone has a talent they're good at. But not everyone knows what it is. Only a lucky few know what theirs are, and sadly, others that don't go to their graves without finding out.

There are plenty of things one can do to ignite a more creative mind-set, which can be valuable in a number of professional and personal situations.

Try everything!

11. Monotasking

People think multitasking is the best way to get things done, but anyone who claims that theory to be true just isn't on the right track anymore.

Monotasking is the new way to be productive, and the best time to start learning how is right now. Choose one task at a time to work on. Only work on that one task for about an hour before taking a break. You can either go back to that task after your break or move on to a different one. The idea is not to jump between multiple smaller tasks at once, which is not good for our brains.

12. Stop Procrastinating

We all struggle with procrastination, myself included. You have no idea how much I've pushed writing this away for "another time." Procrastination has been called many names down the ages: the thief of time, the opportunity's assassin, and the grave in which dreams are buried. It's a habit that sticks itself onto us like Spiderman on a vertical wall. Of course, you can get rid of this bad habit by learning to manage and control your procrastination habits. Stop procrastinating to the point where it's negatively impacting you or other people. Eliminate the distractions and get to work.

13. Stress Management

Stress is everywhere. It's like a living organism within us, feeding up on us. It is the body's reaction to anything that requires a response. Feeling stress can keep us alert and motivate us to pursue our goals. However, if there's too much stress, this can lead to distress. Distress can cause headaches, elevated blood pressure, and chest pain. It can lead you to have problems sleeping and can even make you sick.

Knowing how to manage stress effectively—using good stress to learn and grow, and being able to release stress once it starts to reach a negative level—is vital for personal development.

When you get home after a long day at work, find a way to relieve the stress. What helps you relieve stress? A walk on the beach? Sleeping? Swimming? Meditation? Yoga? Talking? All these are forms to help you battle stress and thereby grow your own self.

14. Compliments

You know how it feels when someone says something nice to you. The feeling is good. Growth is making other people feel good about themselves. Say anything: "You look nice today," "You still make the best coffee." Anything. Make someone feel nice, and you'll be "leveling up" in your personal development.

Compliments make a world of difference.

15. Reduce "I"

When dealing with a confrontation with other people, use "I" less often. It is tempting to use yourself as an example for every piece of commentary you offer up, but it isn't necessary.

Focus less on you and more on that thing you are a part of.

16. Start to Finish

Make a mental note to yourself that, whatever you start, you will finish. Although we might find ourselves with less time and energy, make it a goal that when you start something, you will most definitely finish it.

17. Clear Speech

Be able to speak clearly, and make sure that words are properly enunciated and given the right energy. By doing this, you would be improving your communication skills. Your communication skills are part of your personal brand. Never be lazy in your communication style. How you communicate is vitally important to the advancement of your life and career.

18. Dress Better

Dressing up right is an art one should master. It helps you create a more positive first impression when you meet people. It doesn't necessarily have to be luxurious clothing, but it should involve presenting yourself in a way that projects professionalism and style. You do not have to spend a lot of money to do this. People are skeptical by nature. Never give them a reason not to want to work with you, or do business with you. Present yourself in a manner that makes you approachable. Not only will this help with your self confidence, but you'll be perceived in a much more positive manner.

19. Eating Healthy

You know that saying, "You are what you eat." That is very true. If you don't treat yourself and your stomach right, you won't be in the right shape to achieve your personal and professional goals.

20. Exercise

Energy is the key to productivity, and by exercising regularly, you can boost your energy levels significantly. Start by setting achievable goals, such as walking ten thousand steps per day or getting out of breath at least twice a week.

21. Learn an Instrument
Playing musical instruments is one of those things that help one relax. And coupled with that, it's a load of fun. After a long day, playing an instrument can help you unwind, focus, and improve your brain function, spatial awareness, and coordination.

22. Yoga
You need to do something to those joints of yours and keep the blood pumping. Yoga is known to be one of the most effective and beneficial forms of exercise, and it can be done easily at home using free instructional videos.

23. Improve Your Body Language
Having the right body language can help you in various aspects of your life. It can help you connect better with others and get your message across more effectively. It communicates confidence. It improves your performance.

24. Learn to Get Along Well With Others
Having human relationships is important—not only to grow, but also because it makes us human. Without that connection we get from other people, we would be nothing, like a person stranded on an island alone. Relate to other people, and you'll be opening yourself up to growth. Find that common ground. There is always something you can find in another person that will open up the communication.

25. Become an Early Riser
Develop the habit of getting up early. The age-old proverb that says, "Early to bed and early to rise makes a man healthy, wealthy, and wise!" was coined

owing to the multiple benefits of an early riser. Some of these include watching and enjoying the sunrise, doing some early-morning exercise for your fitness, being able to work on a project just because it's important to you before the day officially gets started, and so on. In addition, studies show that early risers are happier, healthier, and more productive than their late-rising counterparts.

We are at our very best in the morning. For me personally, most of my brilliant ideas come to me very early in the morning. The early morning is when I focus on transformational tasks. The early morning is also when I focus on feeding my mind with positive things such as business books and personal growth books, which develop me as a person and help me to grow and become better.

26. Become More Proactive

You get more things done and do them better if you're proactive. What proactive people do: They don't identify themselves as victims of external conditions. They see themselves as being creators of their lives. They take their own fate into their own hands. And they take responsibility. One of the ways to be proactive is to plan your day so you know exactly what your plan of action will be. Most people wake up in the morning putting fires out or just doing whatever comes their way without structure. Being proactive means you're preventing the fires from happening in the first place. You're either proactive or reactive—and the latter doesn't empower you to succeed. Being proactive is a skill that every successful person I know lives by.

27. Let Go of the Past

Letting go of the past is one of the hardest things for people to do. We are haunted by the ghosts of our past. It's something we all have in us, myself included. And for each person, it's a different thing: the opportunity we missed, what our actions caused in our lives or other people's lives; that person we loved but who didn't love us back, or who loved us but didn't want to be with us; or how we held on too long when we should have let go. Like Robin Schievenersky from the hit series *How I Met Your Mother* once said, "Perhaps it's easier to stick to the past because it's so familiar, and the future seems so uncertain." But in order to be happy in the present, we need to release the ghosts of the past and clear skeletons from the cupboard. All of us have great experiences from our past and some not so great. We often find ourselves focused on the disempowering things from our past as opposed to things that empower us to be better. Learning from past experiences, both good and bad, will give us the fuel to always do better.

Some of you may have heard a story I tell when I am on stage speaking about a friend of mine. She's a great person with great values. She's successful in her business and just one of the kindest people you'll ever meet. Ten years ago she was in a bad relationship. Her boyfriend was verbally abusive, and he was also seeing other women while they were together. She finally had the courage to end the relationship. The challenge is that with every guy she meets, she's focused on what happened in the former relationship. She's met some really nice guys, but she's so focused on the former relationship that she looks for clues to support her suspicions. And sadly, she's usually not satisfied until she finds something negative, which has been a pattern of hers for quite some time.

Whatever you focus on will show up in your life—period! Where your focus goes, your energy flows. If you're driving a car and all you're focused on is, "Oh my goodness, what if I have an accident?" you'll likely have one. Similarly, if you're driving a car and even though you're accelerating and making progress at a very fast speed, you're looking back while doing so, what will happen? You're going to crash. That's how it is when we focus on the past. We're focused on looking back and not forward; even though we think we're moving forward, it's inevitable that we won't succeed.

Let go of the past. It's over. We cannot change it. Thinking we can will drive us insane. If you've failed, that's ok. Just don't repeat the same mistakes that got you to the failure. Our past is our reference guide in our life, and if it's not managed in a way that empowers us, we will be disempowered. So my friend who was in the abusive relationship, I am happy to say, is now happily married. I got her to understand that the past does not equate to her future unless she allows it to. And she chose to let it go, which resulted in her attracting the right person at the right time. I am not taking away from anyone's painful experience from the past. I know how painful life can be, and I understand that things come up in life that are out of our control even when we work hard and do our best to be great people. But we are also naive in believing that bad things only happen to bad people. Bad things happen to good people too. But we must focus on learning from those experiences and use them as motivation to move us forward in life. In this game called life, we are all on different parts of the field; however, it is our responsibility, no matter where we are in the game, to make our life one that is fulfilling.

28. Read More

Read often. Nothing is more powerful than the treasure of knowledge, and the best way to acquire this treasure is to read as much as you can. Knowledge is power. And one of the best ways to get knowledge is by reading. And look at you reading this: you're learning how to develop personally. Gaining new knowledge satisfies our need for competence, which makes us happier.

Research has proved that acquiring new knowledge satisfies an individual's thirst for competence, which makes them eventually happier. You must develop the habit of reading books that will help you to acquire new skills and to polish your existing skills. I know some people do not enjoy reading. That's fine. Listen to audiobooks to motivate you and inspire you. This is key to having the mind-set to succeed. Feed your mind with empowering words that motivate you to take action in achieving your goals. Turn the TV off and use that time to develop yourself. If TV is something you must watch, then watch something of value that helps you grow. One of the easiest ways to change your mind-set for the better is to stop watching the negativity on TV. Read or listen to motivational or educational business audios instead.

29. Overcome Limiting Beliefs

Having limited beliefs traps us in our own self and prevents us from going outside the box and trying new things because of the fear that it won't work out. Identify your limiting beliefs, overcome them, and replace them with positive beliefs that will allow you to achieve what you want from life. Tony Robbins taught me the value of this, and it changed my life forever. During my time with him, he asked a few of us to write down all the limiting beliefs we had that prevented us from succeeding. That was such an easy task for me because I had so many—so many that it scared me. Once I eliminated my limiting beliefs, that's when life changed for me. I found that my limiting beliefs were actually excuses I gave myself not to take action to make my life better. And I truly believed them as well. Here are some of the most common limiting beliefs I hear as I am coaching people from around the world:

1) I do not have enough time.
2) I do not have enough money.
3) I do not have enough education.
4) I'm not smart enough.
5) No one in my family had a business; therefore, the chances of me having one are slim to none.
6) I'm not good enough.
7) No one will like me.
8) I'm too shy.
9) I don't speak well enough.
10) I'm too young.
11) I'm too old.
12) I'm a woman. No one will take me seriously.
13) My family won't approve.
14) I don't have what it takes.
15) I'm just not wired that way.
16) I need at least eight hours of sleep to function.
17) I'm not pretty enough.
18) I'm not tall enough.
19) I'm too busy.
20) It's Impossible.
21) I can't start my own business because I have a job.
22) I can't start my own business because I have children.

Guess what? All of those limiting beliefs listed are *lies*. They are simply 100 percent untrue. I was in pain just writing them for you. They are **not true**! What limiting beliefs do you have that are holding you back? What have you been taught to believe through your life experiences and conditioning that is hindering you from succeeding? Let's see what we can do to replace them.

Assignment:

1) What are the twenty limiting beliefs you currently have in your life and/or business. Write them below:

1)
2)
3)
4)
5)
6)
7)
8)
9)
10)
11)
12)
13)
14)
15)
16)
17)
18)
19)
20)

2) What would it cost you in five years if you continue to have these limiting beliefs?

_____

_____

_____

_____

_____

_____

3) What would you aspire to do if these limiting beliefs weren't a part of your mind-set? Think BIG!

_____

_____

_____

_____

_____

_____

_____

3) What are the twenty NEW empowering beliefs that will replace your limiting beliefs? This is the exciting part. Write as much as you want:

1)
2)
3)
4)
5)
6)
7)
8)
9)
10)
11)
12)
13)
14)
15)
16)
17)
18)
19)
20)

You've just written down the truth! And I want you to believe that with every bone in your body. Now, as you were writing the new beliefs down, you may have heard whispers from your limiting beliefs that the empowering things you wrote down are simply not true. We all hear those voices. It's that little woman or little man sitting on your shoulders telling you that you're not good enough—that everyone else can have it, but not you; that you know you're not good enough to achieve greatness, and you know all the reasons why. Again, these are all lies. Don't listen to them. The good news is that once you condition yourself to think differently, those negative voices will miraculously go away and bother someone else. But it's up to you to recondition your mind-set to think this way.

Take what you've written down and post it somewhere where you can constantly see it. Let it be your daily affirmation. Anything in your life that is taking you away from this type of thinking must be eliminated. Negative people in your life who do not support your goals and aspirations or who belittle them must be removed from your life. You cannot afford to have anyone or anything slow you down. You are worthy and deserving of all the good things coming to you as a result of your new way of thinking. And although bumps in the road are inevitable, you have what it takes to work through them and still sustain your momentum to succeed.

30. Increase Your Willpower

Having willpower is important. It is important to your ability to accomplish anything. Whatever goals you've set for yourself, you need willpower in order to achieve them. Willpower comes from being focused on "why" you must do something as opposed to "how" you do something. When we set goals for ourselves, oftentimes we do not know how to accomplish them. In almost every case, we need the help from those who are experienced in doing what it is we want to do. If we are focused on the "how," we will fail every time because we do not know how in most cases; therefore, we will lose our willpower to continue. When we focus on the "why," it's a game changer. The why is so important because it becomes personal. Your why is your fuel and motivation to take action. You also have an emotional connection with your why that drives you to succeed.

Stop focusing on your how. When your why is strong enough, I promise you that your how will suddenly appear. Whenever you're writing goals for yourself, I want you to make sure you know the why behind those goals. If your why isn't strong enough, there's a possibility that perhaps the goal isn't important enough for you to even accomplish. Your why will also give you clarity, which will result in much stronger willpower to make it happen. Also, focus on the result as opposed to the process to get there. The result is the prize that will, again, give you the motivation to succeed. Without knowing the outcome, oftentimes it's hard to develop the willpower to take action.

31. Work on Your Attitude

Your attitude is your state of mind, the way you process the things around you and respond to them. The only attitude is this: adopt the attitude that is most conducive to getting what you want. Your attitude toward anything in your life directly impacts your result. Your attitude is part of your brand as a person. Bad attitudes usually get bad results, while great attitudes usually get great results. How you show up every day is so important. You must show up at a level ten in everything you do. It's no longer ok to be a level eight because we live in a competitive world, and you must do whatever it takes with the best attitude in order to achieve what you want in life.

Some people wake up in the morning and say, "Why me? Why do I have to go to work?" Your attitude should be, "Why not me?" and you should focus on the fact that you "get" to go to work. Words that we say to ourselves are so important. Our brains listen to everything we tell it, the good and the bad. If you're constantly feeding your brain with negativity, it will show up in your attitude. So be careful what you say to yourself. Always use empowering words.

It is equally important not to listen to someone else's negative opinion of you. That's simply none of your business. Someone else's negative or abusive opinion of you never has to become your reality, unless you allow it to. We've all heard that whom you align yourself with is who you will become, so choose your friends wisely. You are just as special as anyone else. You have more potential than you will ever imagine. You are destined to succeed, and your attitude will play a big part in making that a reality. Focus on all that's good about who you are because there's far more good in you than what's not good. You must believe that!

32. Find Your Passion

Find things that excite you, and go after them. But you can't do this if you're not honest with yourself. So, before you can find that thing that stimulates your interest, be honest with yourself. Every successful person I know has a passion for what he or she does. Whatever you're passionate about or excited about is what drives you. You have to have the passion to succeed. Are you currently passionate about what you do? If the answer is no, you might try reconsidering what it is you're doing.

33. Embrace Your Mistakes

To err is human. But what you should do when you make a mistake is not sulk about it and instead learn from it for future purposes. And every day, as you go on about your day, leave a space in your mind for your mistakes—that will get you prepared for when the mistakes come. The key is to learn from your mistakes and not to repeat them. In life and business, mistakes happen, and to succeed you must be willing to make them. If you're afraid of making them, you'll limit your actions toward achieving your goals. The key is to limit the amount of mistakes you're making.

If you've never had a business or you are having a hard time growing your business, hire a successful business coach to get you there. You can do it yourself and endure the many mistakes you make (and mistakes cost money) or you can align yourself with someone who has done it successfully who can show you the way. You'll still make mistakes, but you're limiting the mistakes you're making by working with someone who has done it over and over again. So, start those goals that you've been putting off because you're afraid of the failure that comes with achieving them. We've all been there, and until you embrace it, you'll never take the necessary action to achieve them.

34. Be Optimistic

Sure, life gives you a load of reasons not to be optimistic. But optimism is great! It makes you see every bad thing from a different angle—it lets you have that thing called hope. By looking at things with a positive outlook, you'll be making yourself more productive and more confident.

By cultivating a relentlessly positive attitude, you can make yourself more productive, more approachable, and more productive. After all, positive things happen to positive people.

35. Embrace Empathy

Empathy is about objectively comprehending differing perspectives, which in turn provides a wealth of insight into your perspective.

36. Listen Actively

Actively learn to pay attention and demonstrate to others that you truly value their opinions and what they have to say. Choose active listening and open-ended questions with supporting body language, and remove any distractions that impede your ability to listen.

37. Make Fear Your Friend

To eliminate fear, you have to first be exposed to fear. Allow yourself to feel afraid and expose yourself to it. Once you are comfortable with the ambiguity and uncertainty of the situation, you can start working your way through it in a calm, rational manner.

38. Improve Your Body Language

Your body language is nothing but nonverbal communication, which includes the gestures and movements you project. Research has proved that the correct body language can help you connect effectively with others and convey your message across more efficiently. It conveys your assertiveness, confidence, and perseverance. In fact, certain body postures can also help to improve your performance.

39. Get Along with Others
You must always look for means to create a rapport with others. However, you need to be honest, and your primary objective should not be to manipulate others. Rather you should learn the ways through which you can relate and get along well with others.

40. Get Along with Yourself
Getting along with yourself is a precursor to getting along with others. You must learn to appreciate and accept your skills, experience, philosophies, aspirations, and limitations. This healthy focus and more grounded "you" will be inspirational and charismatic.

41. Master the Art of Conflict Resolution
Conflict is part and parcel of life. The key is to develop the skill of conflict resolution. If you possess the ability to resolve conflicts rationally and settle disputes amicably, it will certainly make more successful and happy.

Stages Of Personal Development

Personal development, like everything else, has stages. And being aware of the stages is crucial to evolve further into your personal growth and make success yours. Sometimes it's better to delve into a hole without knowing what's on the other side; well, that's not the same with personal development. To be able to understand what personal development truly is, one of the things you must do is know its stages.

Self-growth is a long process—Rome wasn't built in a day—that consists of certain stages of personal development, and knowing the stage you are in is crucial if you want to take another step and move onto the next level.

1. Self-Knowledge

This is the first stage where you start analyzing yourself, figuring out your strengths—and honoring them to improve your personal and professional life—and weaknesses; understanding yourself better; and learning more about what you need and what your goal in life is. Personal development is actually impossible without knowing yourself first—so if you think you can wing it, you're so far from self-growth.

2. Healing

Then comes healing. To be prepared for your growth (which, in other words, is your future), you have to heal your past wounds and traumas and, most importantly, let go of your past failures. It's like when you want to begin sowing a seed in your farm or garden, what is the first thing you do? Prepare the soil by adding fertilizer, manure, water, or new soil. Doing all this has its benefits: the plant will grow fresh and better. Yet some people can't heal on their own. If you're one of these people, there are counselors out there, or even close friends, who will help you get through the hurts of your past.

3. Comparison to Other People

You know that dreadful feeling you get when people compare you to other people who are somehow better than you? Well, with personal development, you *should* compare yourself to other people. Join them in comparing you to other people who are better than you. That way, you can learn from other people: what exactly makes them better than you, more successful than you, and more attractive than you, and what makes you lesser than them—what you have been doing wrong! And you'll find yourself becoming a better you because of the intel you've gained by comparing.

Now, I know we've heard that the only people we should compare ourselves with is ourselves. I never understood that quote. We need to look at others who are doing far better than we are and find out what the components are that we're lacking so that we can be like them. I always look at people who are far more successful than I am and ask myself what they're doing that I can do to better. What are they reading? Where do they go? How is their mind-set different than my mind-set? These are questions I ask myself so that I can improve my life. We cannot accept mediocrity by comparing ourselves to those who are less successful than we are. That will just make us feel better but will not allow us to grow.

I always tell audiences around the world when I am speaking at business conferences that I spend 80 percent of my time around people who are far more successful than I am. Some are shocked when I say this. The reason is because

I want to become better and smarter and more successful. If you're not growing, you are dying. A plant that is nurtured and taken care of will grow, but not nurturing the plant will make the plant die. That said, the opposite of growth is death. If you're not growing your business, it's dying. If you're not growing your health, it's dying. If you're not growing your relationship, it's dying. If you're not growing your finances, they're dying. Without growth you will not find fulfillment. So, aligning yourself with people who are better than you and more successful than you will force you to grow massively.

You are an average of the five people you spend the most time with. Are you spending time with quality people who are encouraging you to grow and succeed? Are they holding you accountable to do so? Are they outstanding examples of the type of person you wish to become? These are the types of questions you must ask, and you must evaluate the people in your life to figure this out.

4. Laying a Strong Foundation

Once you've known what it is you might have been doing wrong, and what makes more successful people better than you, then you can start laying a foundation. It's like an architect's job. An architect won't start the construction of a building unless he checks his design on paper very well before proceeding. And when he realizes he has crossed his t's and dotted his i's, that is when the construction begins. This is basically what this stage is all about. By clarifying things about yourself, you can now set your solid groundwork with a good support system, which is essential for your growth to flourish.

5. Modification

The fifth stage is modification. Look at it this way: after the architect has designed the building perfectly and allowed its construction, and the house has been fully built, before the owners move in, they go in first to take a look around and see how they can modify the style into their own style—for example, where each piece of furniture would go. That's modification: incorporating your stuff the best way into the house. So, when you start thinking about changing your life for better by improving your knowledge, skills, and views, that's where modification begins. Your reason to change may be because of an inspiring talk you heard on Oprah, or a YouTube video, or a film, or even a book, or mainly because you'd just like to incorporate new and better lifestyles into your life.

6. Accepting It

You know what you want in life now. You have finally reached the point in your life where you have decided to begin to live a new and better life. At this stage, you know what you want, you know it might take time for you to get there, but you are still ready to push on. Why? Because it is number six on the list of "Stages of Personal Development." You accept that self-growth is a step-by-step thing; it doesn't just happen overnight. You have accepted who you are, and who you would like to be. This helps you value yourself more.

7. Gaining Maturity

This point is where you develop both mental and emotional maturity during your personal growth. Added to that, you'll find yourself becoming more self-sufficient during this process. Rather than feeling like a victim, blaming others for your problems—allowing yourself to be the victim of circumstances—you'll be feeling instead the empowerment to help yourself. You will also find that you are in a strong and better position to help others.

8. Planning

Ever wondered why there are event planners who oversee weddings, class parties, etc.? It is to make sure things do not go off the rails. Because without plans, what are you doing? There is a high probability that on your way to that place you're heading, you would sleep on it and slide off the path. This is the stage where you plan everything ahead by getting a checklist or a to-do list of things you need to do to get better at being a better person. You number your goals, be they long term or short term, according to their priority and the scale of preference, and you set a deadline. And as you complete the tasks on your list, you mark them off; this gives you a sense of accomplishment, a reason to keep on going.

9. Expansion

The ninth stage is expansion. This is the stage where you get on your way toward becoming that person you want to be. In this stage, you will develop new relationships and friendships and strengthen your networks. These human connections are something we all need to survive: To be able to breathe freely. To be able to feel like we are not just doing this for ourselves; we are also doing it for the people around us to see us in a better light.

10. Patience

At this stage, you'll probably be getting tired. It might even seem to you that you don't seem to be moving forward in your goal. But that's the thing: having that feeling is a sign you're getting close to achieving what you want. A believer would say that at this time the devil is tempting you to stop. But no one wants to listen to the devil, right? Right. So, go on, continue fighting. After all, nothing comes easy, and there is no gain without pain. Think of it this way: you spend hours in the gym every day to achieve that sexy hot body. At a point, you'll feel like stopping altogether. Your body is sore all over, "To hell with a smoking hot body," you might think, but we both know you won't stop. You just need to remember the reason why you're doing it in the first place.

Fight against your doubts and fears, move out of your comfort zone, and work hard, and you'll be able to catch glimpses of the light at the end of the tunnel.

11. Fulfillment

In this stage, you will begin to reap the fruit of your growth. You have successfully moved through all the stages and made them say, "Level complete!" At this stage, you have succeeded in growing as a person; you have checkmated your planned to-do list. And now, your desire to keep developing will start to feel natural and automatic, just like breathing is to you (after all, the sky is the limit, and as much as one wishes it, one can never reach it). And also, your improvement and enhancement continue in your subconscious mind.

Now you're enjoying the realization in your daily life while achieving more and more.

Case Studies Of Successful People

Before I go further, let me talk to you about some of the successful people out there in the world today. At the end of this section, you will realize they all have one thing in common, and perhaps you'll learn from it. I hope so. Stay with me.

1. Ray Kroc (McDonald's)

Raymond Albert "Ray" Kroc was mostly known as an American businessman—specifically in relation to McDonald's. In the 1920s, when Kroc was a little kid, his father made a fortune speculating on land, but in 1929, he lost everything due to the stock market crash. During the Depression, Kroc worked a variety of jobs, ranging from selling paper cups to being a real-estate agent to playing piano in bands. Things began to change, however, when after World War II, Kroc found employment as a milkshake mixer salesman for the food-service-equipment manufacturer Prince Castle. Then, Prince Castle Multi-Mixer sales suddenly plummeted because of competition from lower-priced Hamilton Beach products and because of the high purchase of the product by Richard and Maurice McDonald. It was at this time that Kroc saw the future of the concept and design of this small chain; he saw that it had the potential to expand across the nation, and he believed it, so he visited the McDonald's in 1954. Before Kroc joined McDonald's, he had been in approximately one thousand kitchens, but this time was different. Kroc believed the McDonald brothers had the best-run operation he had ever seen. The restaurant was clean, modern, and mechanized, and the staff were professional and well groomed, but still he saw a better vision for McDonald's.

In 1955, Kroc opened the first McDonald's franchise partnered with the McDonald brothers. Immediately, after finalizing the franchise agreement with the McDonald brothers, Kroc sent a letter to Walt Disney. The two had previously met as ambulance attendant trainees at Sound Beach, Connecticut, during World War I. This is what Kroc wrote in the letter: "I have very recently taken over the national franchise of the McDonald's system. I would like to inquire if there may be an opportunity for a McDonald's in your Disney development." That is a man with a vision.

Unfortunately, that didn't work out. But Kroc pushed on, and in 1960, he became frustrated with the McDonald brothers' desire to maintain a small number of restaurants—the stagnancy galled him. Despite Kroc's pleas, the brothers never sent any formal letters that legally allowed the changes in the chain. And in 1961, Kroc bought the company for $2.7 million—enough to pay each brother $1 million after taxes with the help of his financial wizard Harry Soneborn.

At the time of Kroc's death, the business had 7,500 outlets in the United States and thirty-one other countries and territories. And he was worth $600 million.

Point: a man who came from nothing and started as an ordinary milkshake mixer salesman with a vision and a belief and an unrelenting attitude, built a small restaurant chain into a nationwide and eventually global franchise, making it the most successful fast-food corporation in the world. And the kicker is, he even bought the business from the people he partnered with in the first place.

2. Sir Richard Branson

Branson's dream from his childhood was to become an entrepreneur. Branson first ventured into the world of business when he was sixteen. His first business venture was a magazine called *Student* in which he interviewed different personalities like Mick Jagger and R. D. Laing. He also advertised popular records in the *Student*, and that was an overnight success. He traded under the name

Virgin, and sold records for less than the "High Street" outlets, especially the chain W. H. Smith.

In 1970, Branson set up a mail-order record business and a chain of record stores and called it Virgin Records, which eventually became Virgin Megastores in 1972. He then signed many artists and went on to become the world's largest independent record label.

Branson's Virgin brand grew rapidly during the 1980s, and he set up Virgin Atlantic airline and expanded the Virgin Records music label. He also launched *Virgin Mobile* in 1999, and Virgin Blue in Australia (now renamed Virgin Australia) in 2000.

In 1993, he took a risk and entered the railway business and called his new company Virgin Trains. In 2004, Branson announced the signing of a deal under which a new space tourism company, Virgin Galactic, will license the technology behind Spaceship One to take paying passengers into suborbital space. Next, Branson ventured into the world of oil with Virgin Fuels, which he said was set up to respond to global warming and exploit the recent spike in fuel costs by offering a revolutionary, cheaper fuel for automobiles and, in the near future, aircraft. In 2006, Branson formed Virgin Comics and Virgin Animation, an entertainment company focused on creating new stories and characters for a global audience.

In 2007, a new company was launched with much fanfare and publicity under the name Virgin Media. He also created Virgin Health Bank, which was to give parents the opportunity to store their baby's umbilical-cord-blood stem cells in private and public stem-cell banks. Branson also invested in an 80 percent buyout of Manor Grand Prix, with the team being renamed Virgin Racing. His other business ventures include Virgin Cola, Virgin Cars, Virgin Publishing, Virgin Clothing and Virgin Brides, all of which—unlike the others—failed.

But the point is Branson never gave up. He kept pushing, raising the bar high for himself. In his autobiography, on his decision to create an airline, he wrote: "My interest in life comes from setting myself huge, apparently unachievable, challenges and trying to rise above them…from the perspective of wanting to live life to the full, I felt that I had to attempt it."

And one thing I was waiting to mention at this point is that Branson had dyslexia, which means he had poor academic performances in school. On the last day of school, his headmaster, Robert Drayson, told him he would either end up in prison or become a millionaire. And look how his life ended up. He didn't let this issue stop him, or bring him down. Instead, he went on to become Sir Richard Branson (knighted at Buckingham Palace because of his services to entrepreneurship), an English business magnate, investor, and philanthropist, who founded the Virgin Group, which is responsible for more than four hundred companies. He is valued at $5.1 billion as of November 2017.

3. Ingvar Kamprad

Kamprad was raised on Elmtaryd, a farm in Sweden. When he was five, Kamprad started to sell matches. This was his introduction to the business world. At age seven, when he realized that he could buy the matches in bulk from Stockholm— and with bulk buying comes a cheaper price—and sell them at a low price, and still make a good profit, he began using his bicycle to go further and sell to further neighbors. Later on, he moved into selling dishes, Christmas tree decorations, seeds, pencils, and ballpoint pens. And when he gained a cash reward from his father at seventeen for doing well in his studies, IKEA was founded. Then, he started selling replicas of his uncle's kitchen table. In 1948, he thought about what else to add and then proceeded to add furniture to his portfolio.

With much work under him, he became, in 2010, the eleventh richest person in the world with $23 billion to his name. And his net worth as of February 2016 is believed to be $3.4 billion.

The fact about Kamprad is, he never went to college, and he also had dyslexia. Although rich, throughout his life, Kamprad remained level headed, and humble, and a source of example for his employees to follow—he constantly used himself as an example when talking with IKEA staff. And not only that, he always flew economy class, sat in second-class train cars when possible, never stayed at expensive hotels, recycled tea bags, pocketed salt and pepper packets at restaurants, and also encouraged IKEA employees to use both sides of pieces of paper. In the *Testament of a Furniture Dealer*, Kamprad explained his social philosophy: "It is not only for cost reasons that we avoid the luxury hotels. We don't need flashy cars, impressive titles, uniforms or other status symbols. We rely on our strength and our will!"

Wise words from a wise man.

4. Nick Vujicic

This guy proves that you do not have to have arms or legs to be successful. Born with tetra-amelia syndrome, a rare disorder characterized by the absence of arms and legs. He is one of the seven known surviving individuals planet-wide who live with the syndrome. Today, he is an Australian Christian evangelist and motivational speaker.

Nick has gone through many phases in his life, starting from his own parents. At the time of his birth, his mother refused to see him or hold him while the nurse held him in front of her. As a child growing up on earth, and with this rare condition, he was bullied quite often. Even people who are normal are bullied—now imagine the kind of torture Nick would have gone through at every step of his life from people who surrounded him, who did not understand him, did not see him, or saw him as a freak of nature. Nick attempted suicide in those days. But when asked about it, he would state that he had an amazingly normal childhood. Despite being bullied, he looked on life with positivity and pushed on—and I suppose he indeed had an amazingly normal childhood if you look at it this way. Being bullied didn't set him apart from other kids; in fact, it made him like other kids, seeing as that's how kids treat themselves. Some would argue that was how Nick looked at his life. They wanted to make him feel bad, but he put on a positive attitude, for he saw what that meant.

He started to give talks at his prayer group when he was seventeen after he was shown a newspaper about a man dealing with a severe disability by his mother. In 2005, Nick founded an international nonprofit organization and ministry called Life Without Limbs. And in 2007, he founded Attitude Is Altitude, a secular motivational speaking company.

Nick is well loved by the people who know him. He is known majorly for the inspirational talks he gives, such as the time he spoke during the session "Inspired for a Lifetime" at the World Economic Forum in Davos, Switzerland, on 30 January 2011. And that is not all he has to his name. Nick, at the 2010 Method Fest Independent Film Festival was awarded Best Actor in a Short Film for his performance as Will in the short film *Butterfly Circus*.

In the book he wrote, called *Life Without Limits: Inspiration for a Ridiculously Good Life*, he gave an insight into how his life has been and how whatever anyone is going through should not be a letdown for them. He also markets a DVD for young people titled *No Arms, No Legs, No Worries!*

5. Simon Cowell

Some of you might know him better as the no-nonsense man on the talent hunt shows such as British Got Talent, X Factor, America's Got Talent, American Idol, and Pop Idol.

In his early years, Simon was working for his father in the mail room in EMI Publishing but left after failing to get a promotion to try and look for other things. And we can say that was the best decision of his life—because if he had not, he would not have established E&S Music with his former boss at EMI, which later led him down the road to form Fanfare Records with Iain Burton. His life took a turn for the better when in 1986, a song called *So Macho* by Sinitta became a hit. But then, in 1989, his company began to downspin. He lost everything and nearly became bankrupt. But as a visionary, he did not give up. His career restarted with S Records under BMG when he created novelty records with powerful acts and also a song from two actors whom he convinced to record a song for him. The song became a hit and became UK's number one on the recording chart.

Cowell has been involved in charity work for many years, being generous to people who need it—such as his works as a patron of Together for Short Lives, the leading UK charity for all children with life-threatening and life-limiting conditions, and also the production of the charity single "Everybody Hurts" in aid of victims of the 2010 Haiti earthquake. There is a lot to tell about Simon, and in his book *I Don't Mean To Be Rude, But...*, Simon told the whole story of his childhood.

Now he is worth £325 million.

6. Steve Jobs

There is hardly any educated person in the world who has not heard of Steve Jobs. People know who Steve Jobs is! Even as kids start to grow in age, they start to learn about that person that birthed that gadget they have so often in their hands. He is known mostly as one of the cofounders of Apple Inc. His other ventures include being CEO and the majority shareholder of Pixar and the founder, chairman, and CEO of NeXt. Jobs can be said to be one of the pioneers of the microcomputer revolution.

But how did this journey start?

The first challenge Jobs had to go through in life was growing up knowing his parents gave him up for adoption. In later years, he often classified his biological parents as being only "a sperm bank and an egg bank."

In school, he was often bullied, and they termed him a "socially awkward loner." In a 2005 commencement speech for Stanford University, Jobs stated that during one period, he slept on the floor in friends' dorm rooms, returned Coke bottles for food money, and got weekly free meals at the local Hare Krishna temple. Then, In 1973, Steve Wozniak designed his own version of the classic video game Pong and gave the board to Jobs, who took the game down to Atari, Inc. And because of his sweet talk, Atari gave him a job as a technician. Then, Jobs traveled to India in mid-1974 in search of spiritual enlightenment, and you could say he was enlightened. In 1976, Wozniak invented the Apple I computer and showed it to Jobs, who suggested that they sell it. While they were still starting the business, a neighbor, Larry Waterland, said he dismissed Jobs's budding business: "'You punched cards, put them in a big deck,' he said about the mainframe machines of that time. 'Steve took me over to the garage. He had a circuit board with a chip on it, a DuMont TV set, a Panasonic cassette tape deck and a keyboard. He said, 'This is an Apple computer.' I said, 'You've got to be joking.' I dismissed the whole idea.'" And throughout the whole Apple startup, Steve Jobs didn't get his hands dirty in that sense. Instead, he spent hours on the phone trying to find investors for the company. Then, they received funding from a then-semiretired Intel product marketing manager and engineer.

Jobs ripped Silicon Valley apart. Why? Because he'd created a very successful company at a young age.

Jobs and Apple became more successful when Apple went public, and Jobs became a millionaire. Jobs was worth a million dollars when he was twenty-three in 1978, ten million when he was twenty-four, and over a hundred million when he was twenty-five. He was also one of the youngest "people ever to make the Forbes list of the richest people in the United States—and one of only a handful to have done it themselves, without inherited wealth."

7. Oprah Winfrey

Oprah is one of the most popular women in the world today and has been labeled the richest African American, the greatest black philanthropist in American history, and North America's first multibillionaire black person. Several assessments rank her as the most influential woman in the world. But if you look at where she started from, your jaw would drop and a tear might probably fall.

Winfrey was born into poverty in rural Mississippi to a teenage single mother, and her first six years on earth were spent with her grandmother, who was indeed poor—so poor that sometimes Oprah had to wear dresses made of potato sacks, for which the local children bullied her and made fun of her.

Oprah stated that she was molested growing up by people closest to her— her cousin, her uncle, and a family friend. Oprah ran away from home when she was thirteen because she could not take any more of the abuse. And at fourteen, she became pregnant, but her son—God bless his soul—was born prematurely and died shortly after birth.

When Oprah was in high school, she became an honors student and was voted Most Popular Girl. She then joined her high school speech team at East Nashville High School, placing second in the nation in a dramatic interpretation. She won an oratory contest, which secured her a full scholarship to Tennessee State University, where she studied communication. When she was seventeen, Winfrey won the Miss Black Tennessee beauty pageant, which attracted the attention of the local black radio station, WVOL, which then hired her to do the news part time. She worked there during her senior year of high school, and again while in her first two years of college.

In 1983, Winfrey relocated to Chicago to host WLS-TV's low-rated half-hour morning talk show, *AM Chicago*. Within months after Oprah took over, the show went from the last place in the ratings to overtaking *Donahue* as the highest-rated talk show in Chicago. The movie critic Roger Ebert persuaded her to sign a syndication deal with King World. Ebert predicted that she would generate forty times as much revenue as his television show, *At the Movies*. *AM Chicago* was then renamed *The Oprah Winfrey Show*. Oprah's attitude toward life brought in double *Donahue*'s national audience, displacing *Donahue* as the number-one daytime talk show in America. *TIME* magazine once wrote:

Few people would have bet on Oprah Winfrey's swift rise to a host of the most popular talk show on TV. In a field dominated by white males, she is a black female of ample bulk. As interviewers go, she is no match for, say, Phil Donahue…What she lacks in journalistic tough-ness, she makes up for in plainspoken curiosity, robust humour and, above all, empathy. Guests with sad stories to tell are apt to rouse a tear in Oprah's eye…They, in turn, often find themselves revealing things they would not imagine telling anyone, much less a national TV audience.

In the mid-1990s, Winfrey adopted a less tabloid-oriented format, hosting shows on broader topics such as heart disease, geopolitics, spirituality, and meditation; interviewing celebrities on social issues they were directly involved with, such as cancer, charity work, or substance abuse; and hosting televised giveaways, including shows where every audience member received a new car (donated by General Motors) or a trip to Australia (donated by Australian tourism bodies). On January 1, 2001, Winfrey and Discovery Communications changed the Discovery Health Channel into a new channel called OWN: Oprah Winfrey Network.

Oprah has, of course, had different emotional problems throughout her rise to greatness. She once wrote a suicide note, to her best friend, Gayle King; she had other emotional troubles too, which led to a weight problem.

The point that this woman, who came out from nothing, raised herself up, kept going, and didn't stop, and now, she's one of the most beloved people on the planet and the richest African American woman. She became a millionaire at the age of thirty-two when her talk show received national syndication. At the age of forty-one, Winfrey had a net worth of $340 million. Now, her net worth is $3 billion. And what's more? She's so respected for her work, there has been a course taught at the University of Illinois focusing on Winfrey's business acumen, namely "History 298: Oprah Winfrey, the Tycoon." And also the *Wall Street Journal* coined the term "Oprahfication," meaning public confession as a form of therapy.

Her memoir, *The Life You Want*, was scheduled for publication in 2017.

8. Coco Chanel

Chanel was known for her lifelong determination, ambition, and energy, which she applied to her professional and social life. She both achieved financial success as a businesswoman and catapulted to social prominence in French high society, thanks to the connections she made through her work. These included many artists and craftspeople to whom she became a patron. Her social connections appeared to encourage a highly conservative personal outlook.

When Chanel was twelve, her mother died of tuberculosis. Then, her father sent his children far away from home. He sent Chanel and her two other sisters to the Corrèze, in central France, to the convent of Aubazine, which ran an orphanage. The orphanage was founded to care for the poor and rejected, which including running homes for abandoned and orphaned girls. "It was a stark, frugal life, demanding strict discipline."

Despite the tragedy of this situation, the orphanage was the place that jumpstarted Chanel's professional life, for it was here she learned to sew.

At eighteen years old, Chanel was considered too old for the orphanage, so they sent her to live in a boarding house set aside for Catholic girls in the town of Moulins. When not working the needle, she was singing in a cabaret frequented by cavalry officers. She was quite the star at La Rotonde, a café concert. She was among other girls dubbed *poseuses*, the performers who entertained the crowd between star turns. As a café entertainer, Chanel radiated a juvenile allure that tantalized the military habitués of the cabaret.

While working at La Rotonde, Chanel met the young French ex-cavalry officer and wealthy textile heir Étienne Balsan. And at age twenty-three, Chanel was already Balsan's mistress. For the next three years, she lived with him in his château Royallieu near Compiègne, an area known for its wooded equestrian paths and the hunting life. It was a lifestyle of self-indulgence; Balsan's wealth and leisure allowed the cultivation of a social set. Balsan lavished Chanel with the beauties of "the rich life"—diamonds, dresses, and pearls.

In 1908, Chanel began an affair with one of Balsan's friends, Captain Arthur Edward "Boy" Capel. Capel, a wealthy member of the English upper class, installed Chanel in an apartment in Paris and financed her first shops. It was at this shop that Chanel introduced several deluxe casual clothes suitable for leisure and sport. The fashion clothes were constructed from humble fabrics such as jersey and tricot, at the time primarily used for men's underwear. Here, Chanel sold hats, jackets, sweaters, and the marinière, the sailor blouse.

But it was when she was with Balsan that she had started designing hats. This was started as a form of diversion, but like all good things, it evolved into a commercial enterprise. She became a licensed milliner in 1910 and opened a boutique named Chanel Modes. Her business, however, didn't start to bloom until actress Gabrielle Dorziat wore her hats in Fernand Nozière's play *Bel Ami* in 1912. And then Dorziat modeled Chanel's hats again in photographs published in *Les Modes*.

In 1921, she opened what may be considered an early incarnation of the fashion boutique, featuring clothing, hats, and accessories and later expanded to offer jewelry and fragrances. By 1927, Chanel owned five properties on the rue Cambon.

In 1921, while in Monte Carlo, Chanel became acquainted with Samuel Goldwyn. She was introduced through a mutual friend, the Grand Duke Dmitri Pavlovich, cousin to the last czar of Russia, Nicolas II. Goldwyn offered Chanel a tantalizing proposition. For the sum of a million dollars (approximately seventy-five million in twenty-first-century valuation), he would bring her to Hollywood twice a year to design costumes for MGM stars. Chanel accepted the offer.

9. Walt Disney

Whenever I see this logo on my screen as I put on the TV, something in me always lights up. Walt Disney is one of the best things out there. Walter Elias Disney developed his interest in drawing when he was paid to draw the horse of a retired neighborhood doctor. Disney also practiced drawing by copying the front-page cartoons of Ryan Walker. At this time, Disney also began to develop an ability to work with watercolors and crayons. When Disney was attending Benton Grammar School, he met fellow student Walter Pfeiffer, who came from a family of theatre fans and introduced Disney to the world of vaudeville and motion pictures. Before long, he was spending more time at the Pfeiffers' house than at home.

Elias had purchased a newspaper delivery route for the *Kansas City Star* and *Kansas City Times*. Disney and his brother Roy woke up at 4:30 every morning to deliver the *Times* before school and repeated the round for the *Evening Star* after school. The schedule was exhausting, and Disney often received poor grades after falling asleep in class, but he continued his paper route for more than six years. He attended Saturday courses at the Kansas City Art Institute and also took a correspondence course in cartooning.

Disney enrolled at McKinley High School and became the cartoonist for the school newspaper, drawing patriotic pictures about World War I. He also took night courses at the Chicago Academy of Fine Arts.

After forging the date of birth on his birth certificate, he joined the Red Cross in September 1918 as an ambulance driver. He was shipped to France but arrived in November, after the armistice. He drew cartoons on the side of his ambulance for decoration and had some of his work published in the army newspaper *Stars and Stripes*.

Then, Disney returned to Kansas City in 1919, where he worked as an apprentice artist at the Pesmen-Rubin Commercial Art Studio. There, he drew commercial illustrations for advertising, theater programs, and catalogs. He also befriended fellow artist Ub Iwerks. With Ub Iwerks, Walt developed the character Mickey Mouse, which turned out to be one of the things that make childhood memories.

In the 1950s, Disney expanded into the amusement park industry, and in 1955 he opened *Disneyland*. To fund the project, he diversified into television programs, such as *Walt Disney's Disneyland* and *The Mickey Mouse Club*. In 1965, he began development of another theme park, Disney World, the heart of which was to be a new type of city, the "Experimental Prototype Community of Tomorrow" (EPCOT). Disney was a heavy smoker throughout his life and died of lung cancer in December 1966 before the park and EPCOT project were completed.

Disney was a shy, self-deprecating, and insecure man in private, but he adopted a warm and outgoing public persona. He had high standards and high expectations of those with whom he worked. Although there have been accusations that he was racist or anti-Semitic, they have been contradicted by many who knew him. His reputation changed in the years after his death, from a purveyor of homely patriotic values to a representative of American imperialism. He nevertheless remains an important figure in the history of animation and in the cultural history of the United States, where he is considered a national cultural icon. His film work continues to be shown and adapted; his studio maintains high standards in its production of popular entertainment, and the Disney amusement parks have grown in size and number to attract visitors in several countries.

A pioneer of the American animation industry, he introduced several developments in the production of cartoons. As a film producer, Disney holds the record for most Academy Awards earned by an individual, having won twenty-two Oscars from fifty-nine nominations. He was presented with two Golden Globe Special Achievement Awards and an Emmy Award, among other honors. Several of his films are included in the National Film Registry by the Library of Congress.

(Source: www.wikipedia.com)

Lessons Learned from These Case Studies

* One of the things we learn from these stories is that having a good education and background doesn't necessarily mean you're going to be successful. But that's not to say education is not important. What I'm saying instead is this: if you do not have an education, it shouldn't be seen as a life-ending issue.
* Successful people never allow themselves to be a victim of their circumstances. They either use those circumstances as a ladder to climb up or learn from it for future purposes.
* Successful people see failure as being something they have to experience on their way to being successful. Failure to them is something to accept when it comes into their path. That mentality makes them prepared for it, not afraid of it or willing to let it stop them from moving forward like several of the people mentioned above.

* They don't let "No" be an answer. They finish what they started. They have the persistency to follow things through. And they do not let the negativity of other people affect their positivity.
* Successful people have the ability to focus on what they want and stick with it. "As a result, they understand that if they focus on what they want and bring that into their conscious awareness then that will become their reality. This ability to be absolutely consciously aware and to think about thinking is a major asset to successful people."
* Dreaming big is something successful people are good at, as well as envisioning a good outcome from it. Having big goals lights a flame in them, making them push harder and faster. And they also live their lives as if they're already where they want to be—achieving that dream of theirs.
* Successful people are no strangers to handling uncertainty. They're flexible that way. They adapt quickly to whatever circumstances arise. And they often see opportunities where others do not.
* Successful people take risks. They don't find reasons not to do it; they find solutions. At times when others would have said, "I can't do this," they see the opportunity. That could either be fruitful or bad, but there's no reward without risk.
* And lastly, they don't let any form of disability disarm them from pursuing their goals. Again, they don't let themselves become a victim of their circumstances.

Origin Of Personal Development

The major religions, such as the Abrahamic and Indian religions, and the modern-day philosophies have used practices like prayer, music, dance, singing, chanting, poetry, writing, sports, and martial arts, as links to the final goals of personal development, such as discovering the meaning of life or living the good life.

In *The Care of the Self*, Michel Foucault describes the techniques of epimelia used in ancient Greece and Rome, which included dieting, exercise, sexual abstinence, contemplation, prayer, and confession, some of which also became important practices within different branches of Christianity as a form of personal development.

In yoga, a discipline originating in India, over three thousand years ago, personal-development techniques include meditation, rhythmic breathing, stretching, and postures.

Yi Wushu and T'ai chi Ch'uan utilize traditional Chinese techniques, including breathing and energy exercises, meditation, and martial arts, as well as practices linked to traditional Chinese medicine, such as dieting, massage, and acupuncture, as forms of personal development.

In Islam, which arose almost 1,500 years ago in the Middle East, personal development techniques include ritual prayer, recitation of the Qur'an, pilgrimage, fasting, and *tazkiyah* (purification of the soul).

Aristotle and Confucius stand out as major sources of what has become personal development in the twenty-first century, representing a Western tradition and an East Asian tradition.

In his *Nicomachean Ethics*, Aristotle defined personal development as a category of *phronesis* or practical wisdom, where the practice of virtues leads to happiness or, put more accurately, living well. Aristotle continues to influence the Western concept of personal development to this day, particularly in the economics of human development and positive psychology.

(Source: www.wikipedia.com)

Change

Aside from death, change is an inevitable aspect of life. Change is an ingredient of life no one can run away from. Be it positive or negative, change exhibits itself in the life of every individual. Like we all know, change is an integral part of success. To achieve success, a person has to change certain aspects of his life in order to embrace the bigger change coming his way.

But as easy and inevitable as change sounds, humans still cringe at the sound of the word. Humans are creatures of habit. When they get used to something, the idea of a change sends shock waves through their spines. "Will I be able to do this under another atmosphere?" "Am I financially stable enough to change my job?" "Can I ever stop working with this company?"

Without change, some of the world's biggest companies might still be struggling financially. AT&T started out as a telephone network operator. But at the advent of evolving markets, the company transformed itself into a global provider of Internet carrier services. Sony also began as a recording equipment company. Today, it is known as one of the largest media companies in the whole world.

But positive change is what we should all strive for. Besides the financial prowess and popularity success comes with, positive change allows for happiness, better decision making, and a chance to become better than one already is.

To achieve positive change, there are lifestyles and habits you need to completely drop. Before we look at how one can achieve positive change, let us look at the habits and behaviors we should give up before embarking on the long road to change.

1. Give up the unhealthy lifestyle: As Jim Rohn said, "Take care of your body. It is the only place you have to live." Health is wealth. For you to achieve anything, you must start with your physical health. You have to take care of your health in order to pursue any career that would eventually lead to success. To enforce change, develop yourself and do all sorts of activities; you have to possess good health. You should have a healthy diet. Eat good food. Eat fruits and vegetables. Avoid an addictive use of alcohol and cigarettes. Also, engage in a ton of physical activities. Exercise your body and mind. Meditate. These might look like small steps, but soon they will pay off.

2. Focus more on long-term goals: Successful people are known to set long-term goals. But long-term goals are a result of the short-term goals they put in place, which they need to do every day.

3. Stop making excuses: Making excuses portrays any individual as an irresponsible personality. Successful people understand that they are responsible for their lives, that they are responsible for their actions. In spite of their weaknesses and past failures, these people stood up to face those setbacks and subsequently made the most of the the great personalities they have grown to be.

    You should realize that you are responsible for what happens in your life. This could be frightening and surprisingly exciting at the same time. But it is one of the candid ways you can train yourself to become successful. You should own and take charge of your life, because no one else will.

4. Give up on the fixed mind-set: A fixed mind-set is one that is averse to change. You should possess a fluid and flexible mind-set that changes as the situation demands. People with fixed mind-sets are prone to believing in their intelligence or talents. They believe these qualities alone

can lead them to success, even without hard work. Successful people know the importance of possessing a flexible mind. They invest a great amount of time into developing a growth mind-set, getting new knowledge, learning new skills, and also improving their perceptions of the operations of the world around them.

5. Learn to say no to things that don't support your goals: Successful people understand that for them to keep being at the top of their game, there are certain tasks, activities, and even friends they have to say no to. It could be demands from friends or family members. But they understand that its immediate satisfaction might go a long way in harming their goals, so they simply say no to it.

6. Give up the toxic people in your life: Jim Rohn says, "You are the average of the five people you spend the most time with." The people we spend our time with unconsciously add up to who or what we become. Having toxic and unproductive people in your life gradually makes you an unproductive person.

These people are less accomplished than you are, both in your personal and professional lives, but there are also many others who have achieved more than you have. If you spend time with the ones whose achievements don't measure up to yours, there are great chances you would remain stagnant, or depreciate your value. But when you spend time with those who know and have achieved more than you have, there are better chances of you improving and getting higher up the ladder of complete success.

How To Achieve Positive Change

As I mentioned earlier, it is totally natural to resist change. But change is good for our physical and professional entities. The idea of change leads to more opportunities.

To make an effective positive change in your life, here are powerful tips that can instigate the change you so crave.

1. Identify and understand that thing you want to have changed in your life: Before you can enforce change in your life, or an organization, you must first understand why you want to make that change. Is there a habit you'd like to stop? Is there a "ritual" of activities at work no one wants to break but which is killing the progress of the company? Is there something about you that you really want changed?

    Associate Professor Anthony Grant, from the University of Sydney's Coaching Psychology Unit, states that you should identify your core values and things that are very important to you.

    "You need to be able to identify what it is about your goal that adds to you as a person, that makes you feel better and more expansive," Professor Grant says.

When your goals align with your core values, the mere thought of it would inspire a positive vibe in you.

2. Set a daring goal: Every journey toward change should be preceded by a challenge and an undying passion to get it done. But there's the problem of self-doubt, the moments of "Can I really do this?" When you successfully strip away those blinders, think of the great advantage that would come your way if you took that step toward that goal. Write the goal down in a journal. Keep track of your little successes along the way. Assess the steps you make, and soon a profound liberating experience will soak your whole body.

3. Be more positive: Positivity exudes joy. Being optimistic boosts your mental and physical health. Being surrounded by negativity causes one to never see the good in anything. How is it then possible to have a successful and joyful life?

   Negative people get more stressed, get sick more, and make bad use of the few opportunities they get. Chris Talambas says on *Lifehacker*, "When we make a decision to become positive, and follow that decision up with action, we will begin to encounter situations and people that are more positive."

   Chris understands that being positive isn't easy. That's why he suggests seven ways you can achieve positivity:
   * Be grateful for everything.
   * Laugh more often, especially at yourself.
   * Help others.
   * Change how you think.
   * Surround yourself with positive people.
   * Approach problems with positive actions and solutions.
   * Take full responsibility and stop playing the victim.

4. Be kind to others: Sonja Lyubormirsky, a professor at the University of California, Riverside, says, "People who engage in kind acts become happier over time. When you are kind to others, you feel good as a person— more moral, optimistic and positive."

Also, this was written by the Sufi teacher Hazrat Inayat Khan (1882–1927): "A person who, alone, has seen something beautiful, who has heard something harmonious, who has tasted something delicious, who has smelt something fragrant, may have enjoyed it, but not completely. The complete joy is in sharing one's joy with others. For the selfish one who enjoys himself and does not care for others, whether he enjoys things of the earth or things of heaven, his enjoyment is not complete."

You can be kind to numerous people in countless ways. Purchase a cup of coffee for a stranger in the diner. Visit an old friend. Help out with environmental work. Smile more at people. This way, you are building positive change in yourself by just being your kind self.

5. Build or join a support group or network: According to the Mayo Clinic, "A strong social network can be critical to help you through the stress of tough times, whether you've had a bad day at work or a year filled with loss or chronic illness."

   The importance of social meetings when you are striving to positively change yourself cannot be overemphasized. This group could be made of friends, family members, or strangers dealing with the same problem. Whatever problem you might be going through and finding it hard to break through with a change, now there's a support group somewhere willing to have you in their midst.

   Support groups provide one with a sense of belonging, an increase in self-worth, and also a feeling of security. There's also the assurance that they are there when you need advice or encouragement to avoid slipping back into the habit.

6. Take baby steps. Progress slowly and steadily: Change doesn't happen in a day, or a week. It could take months or years, depending on the amount of energy you put into it. According to John Brubaker, baby steps motivate us to persevere. That perseverance is what trains us to give ourselves more time to deal with ourselves and enforce that change.

Document and celebrate your wins. Document your failures. Reflect on the mistakes. Work against them reoccurring. These will help you achieve that change that you've been seeking in a positive and meaningful way.

Time And Time Management

Time is the ultimate secret of every successful person out there. There are twenty-four hours in a day, but they plan it so well, it eventually looks like thirty-six hours to an average observer. Effective time-management skills prevent you from working the whole day and still complaining that the Earth should have rotated more slowly, so you would earn more hours. But working round the clock would eventually lead to a burnout. And with a burned-out life, success can't be around the corner.

To effectively grasp the idea of this chapter, you have to understand whether you are working too much or not. Do you lose your enthusiasm at the sight of work that once made you smile? Do you no longer feel positively overwhelmed to take up that project and get it over with? Do you feel mentally and physically tired at the end of the day, and still can't get yourself to sleep when you enter the bedroom? Do normal things suddenly seem like work to you?

If you answer yes to most of these questions, then it is obvious you are working too hard and not effectively managing your time. Even worse, this clearly shows that you aren't enjoying your job, and also your life. And it is only a little time before you pack up. The solution to this is simply effective time management. Real time management involves managing your life well, so that you still have the time to sit and stare, because that's when we have the most creative ideas.

Here are seven rules for an effective time management:

1. Always start your day right: Nothing beats a great start. Try as much as possible not to rush into the day. Rushing allows for a lack of composure, which leads to unsuccessfulness. Every morning, take a few minutes to gather your thoughts, goals, and objectives for the day. Highlight and try to remember them as you go round your activities for the day. Also, prepare your mind to be ready for whatever the day brings, whether negative or positive.

2. Break large tasks into reasonable and tiny units: Overwhelming yourself with large tasks hasn't ever been a good idea, and infusing it into your practice doesn't change its negativity. Big tasks can make you feel overwhelmed and hopeless. This way, you spend more time worrying about how to go about the task rather than just solving it. This enormous task also makes it impossible for you to do other valuable things that you need to do.

    Instead, these tasks should be broken down into tiny, achievable bits. This way, you know what it is you want to get done in two hours, in a day, or in a week. Time has become your ally through this; you work hand in hand and avoid the demerits of poor time management.

3. Learn to prioritize: It is usually an enviable skill to be able to discern whether an activity is healthy for you or your business. You should be able to decide the best order in which to do things. You should draw your scale of preferences and not allow the hands of time to draw them for you. You should know the things that need to be done at certain times and the ones that can be done in the future. There are also the ones you can simply forget about, the ones you can say no to.

    You should also learn to reject proposals that you believe wouldn't be of any help to you. This involves saying no to people who want you to do things that you don't have time for.

4. Plan: Planning is the ultimate secret to managing time. Besides its ability to make you seem flawless to other people, with your head always above them, planning gives you the needed time to achieve that goal in spite of the limited time available to you. Planning is the art of scheduling your activities so that you can achieve your objectives and priorities in the time you have available.

   When you effectively schedule your activities, it helps you to:
   a. Have enough time to spend on more personal activities, hence speeding up your pace to personal development and improvement.
   b. Avoid wasting time on frivolous activities.
   c. Work steadily and speedily toward your personal and career goals.
   d. Have enough time to spend with friends and family.
   e. Understand the intricacies of time, and how you can make the best of it.
   d. Ultimately achieve a good work-life balance.

But how do we effectively plan? Do we have to draw a table of plans? A timetable? What exactly do we have to do?

   I. Have your goal in mind: The main reason why you are planning is to achieve something. It is important that no matter how hard or easy it is, that reason should always resonate in the back of your mind. It is probable that plans might change along the line, leading you to change some aspects of your goals. But the bigger picture should remain painted on the walls of your heart.

   II. Write it down: There's a unique thing about writing things down: they are physical manifestations of the things in your mind. Following them involves following your mind. Writing it down makes it real and adds tinges of motivation to whatever it is you want to achieve. Writing gives you the ability to visualize your goals, and this gives you a clearer perspective.

   You can make notes and paste them on the fridge. You can also get a journal or a diary where you take your time to plan out each day (more like a timetable). When you eventually get used to it, all you have to do plan weeks ahead.

III. List your study tasks: Create a long list of all the things you want to get down and the time you have to get them down. You could simply mark dates on the calendar for remembrance. After creating the list, arrange the tasks according to their level of priorities and the time needed to complete each one. These are very simple steps: list, prioritize, and estimate.

IV. Plan frequent breaks: The body needs rest. There are times you will realize you feel like you are under a lot of pressure. At these moments, always take breaks. Go for a walk. Your brain needs time to process and store information.

Most importantly, breaks help relieve stress and enhance motivation. Inadvertently, they keep your physical health in check.

5. Learn to delegate tasks: Delegation of tasks is a quality of every company out there. If you have the capacity to get people to get things done on your behalf, do so. Make sure they are professionals in that field. That way, you don't get burned out doing something you aren't very good at.

Also, they are humans too; encourage them. Tell them they are good at what they do. Continually motivate them.

6. Learn to relax: If you fail to meet a big deadline, or lose out on a big contract, the world isn't going to end. Working round the clock isn't going to bring back what you have lost. You need to cut yourself some slack. Even if you have to force yourself to take time off, do it! The world doesn't revolve around you. Bask in the beauty of the rising sun. Smile. Go on vacation.

7. End each day with a plan for the next day: After critically assessing your day, your decisions, and achievements, create a plan for the next day. It could be an hour-by-hour plan. This gives you a head start on the day. When others are trying to get out of bed, you are midway into completing a whole day's tasks.

How To Effectively Execute Goals

Goals belong to everyone because everyone has one. The achievement of goals is what makes success, no matter its different definition to each person. You could be the CEO of the richest company in the world, and there would still be territories you would look forward to conquering. Those are goals. Goals are borne out of passion for something, an undying zeal to see that thing happen. But goals without a reasonable plan put forward to achieve them could simply pass for a dream. Just a dream. A goal involves plans, commitments, and strategies that will ensure the goal becomes a reality.

Goal setting is a process of deciding what you want to accomplish and devising a plan to achieve the result you desire.

In addition, before you completely seal it off as a goal, there are ways you can check to see if you have a good shot at accomplishing such goal. You must have heard of the SMART acronym, which strives to define the basic qualities every goal should possess.

S—Specific. The goal should be a particular thing you'd like to achieve. It shouldn't be a myriad of ambiguous ideas. For example, I want to start my own company in three years.

M—Measurable. Concrete criteria should be able to be created for measuring progress toward the attainment of each goal you set.

A—Attainable. A goal must be something attainable, achievable. The blog, *Top Achievement*, writes,

> When you identify goals that are most important to you, you begin to figure out ways you can make them come true. You develop the attitudes, abilities, skills, and financial capacity to reach them. You begin seeing previously overlooked opportunities to bring yourself closer to the achievement of your goals.
>
> You can attain most any goal you set when you plan your steps wisely and establish a time frame that allows you to carry out those steps. Goals that may have seemed far away and out of reach eventually move closer and become attainable, not because your goals shrink, but because you grow and expand to match them. When you list your goals you build your self-image. You see yourself as worthy of these goals, and develop the traits and personality that allow you to possess them.

R—Realistic. A goal must represent an objective that you are willing and able to work toward. You can't become a politician today and expect yourself to be the president the next year. Your goal should represent something realistic in your life, and in the world.

T—Timely. Without a specific time frame for your goals, it is impossible to properly measure them. Every goal should have a time limit.

Importance Of Setting Goals

1. Goals give you focus: A human without a goal is equivalent to a polythene nylon picked by the wind that blows as the wind wishes. It is possible to have potential, but potential without a sense of direction is useless. When you set goals, you give yourself a direction, a target you have to meet.

2. Goals keep you undistracted: It is easy to get carried away by the happenings in the world. Goals build mental boundaries around you. The focus a goal gives you is what makes you avoid distractions and keep your eyes on the big picture.

3. Goals make it easy to measure progress: With goals, you are able to know how much you have achieved in a stipulated period of time. They also provide you a benchmark to compare with. When you compare, you know how much you have done and how much effort you need to put in.

4. Goals help you overcome procrastination: Everybody procrastinates, from the most diligent student to the most hardworking businessperson. Procrastination is a monster we have yet to conquer. It is choosing that which you can do now to do at a later date. But when you set a goal, you become accountable to yourself. You report to yourself, chastise yourself. This fills you with a never-felt dose of responsibility. You are

now accountable to yourself to make that task a reality at the chosen time.

5. Goals fill you with motivation: Goals are what provide the drive, the passion to continue pursuing. By making a goal you give yourself a concrete endpoint to aim for and get excited about. It gives you something to focus on and put 100 percent of your effort into and this focus is what develops motivation. Goals are simply tools to focus your energy in positive directions; these can be changed as your priorities change, news ones are added, and others are dropped.

Now we are back to the ultimate question: How do I efficiently make my goals work out? How do I make them become a reality? At this stage, it is believed that your goals meet the SMART criteria. So we'll dive straight into how you can achieve these goals.

1. Commit to your goals: You have to dedicate yourself to the goal you have chosen if you want to accomplish it. That's why it is usually advised to write down your goals. Continually seeing these goals acts as the first step to eventually committing yourself to them. You should understand that accomplishing a goal isn't something that happens overnight. There would be setbacks, failures. But with commitment, these should spur you to keep on trying until you achieve it.

2. Publicize your goal: Making your goal public is a technique that has proven to work in recent years. It is a really effective technique for many people. The fact that most people know about their goals and are monitoring their progress and results ensures commitment and an undying zeal to make sure the goal becomes a reality. You can broadcast it on social media platforms. You could also have a "goal buddy" whom you share your progress and failures with. But this person should be someone sincerely interested in your efforts, who would like to see the fruition of that goal.

3. Set deadlines: Every goal should contain deadlines. Even with the bashings of deadlines by some psychologists in recent times, if planned right

they can make the goal more attainable. Deadlines help shape your plan of action. With deadlines, you have a fixed time frame. Your activities soon border around this time, making you probably achieve the goal before the stipulated time.

4. Reward yourself after accomplishments: A little celebration does no harm. After an accomplishment, celebrate yourself. Celebrate your success. You have devoted a lot of time and effort to success, so you deserve to celebrate it when it eventually comes through. Also, do not undermine your achievement by rewarding yourself in a small way. Know the right reward for the occasion.

5. Make your goals real to you: Susan Ward writes on *The Balance*, "Goal setting is basically a way to approach the process of accomplishment. It's a very successful way, if done right, but like all such processes, it's a bit abstract. Using techniques such as visualization to focus on what actually accomplishing your goal will be like and what it will do for you can be very powerful—and a great help in staying motivated. Choosing and posting pictures that represent successfully accomplishing your goal is another way of doing this."

6. Evaluate your goals: Evaluation gives you an objective way to look at your achievements and the pursuits of your goals. Evaluation allows you to know where you stand so you can know where you need to go. Evaluation creates a baseline for you to work from. It is important to note that evaluation goes hand in hand with reflections.

   Whether a goal was successfully executed or not, there's always a lesson to learn. It is paramount to find out these lessons. Study them. Understand them. Avoid making the mistakes you made before. These lessons will increase your accomplishments as you apply them to your future goals.

7. Build your competence: Competence in this context encompasses the skills, systems, processes, and tools you need to execute your goals. The end result is to make sure you hit your targets.

   Train yourself in your field. Learn more. Expand your horizons. Become a better person and see how it all works with your goals.

Most people set goals for themselves once a year, and that time of year is usually January. Most people check in to see how they're progressing with their goals a year later—and by then it is too late, and the goal is long forgotten. The word goal by definition is the result or achievement toward which effort is directed. A goal without action is meaningless, and it is also very important that you're taking the right action necessary to reach the goal. The right action means doing the right things in the right order so that you get the result you're seeking.

Where most people fail in setting goals in their business or personal life is the disbelief that the goal is achievable—limiting beliefs that set us up to fail before the goals are even written down. Limiting beliefs are the toxic thoughts we tap into as an excuse not to take action. Limiting beliefs are sometimes a result of our conditioning, past experiences, people we align ourselves with, etc.

There are four steps to goal setting that will move you toward your goals. But before these steps are even initiated, you must have the mind-set that failure is not an option and you will achieve what you set out to do. More than 80 percent of everything we do is based on our mind-set. We must adjust our way of thinking before we do anything, and once we do, we will have the fuel necessary to not only take on tasks, but also to sustain our momentum.

1. Make the Decision

Adopting the mind-set that you have made the decision that this is a goal that you must and will accomplish gets you out of the gate with momentum. The decision is the belief that YES you can do this and you WILL do this—no matter the cost. You have now stepped outside of your comfort zone, and this is where the growth begins. Decision by definition is cutting off any other option—YOU have decided! Once you make the decision in your mind to do something, you immediately tap into being resourceful and finding ways to make the goal a reality.

2. Be Committed!

Being committed to anything means you are laser focused, and nothing can make you take your eye off the ball. You must use everything you have and do everything you can, and when you think you are out of fuel, keep pushing forward. Do what you say you're going to do and raise your standards higher than ever before. Get the word "try" out of your vocabulary. Start telling yourself that you WILL do what you say you'll do. People who usually fail do so by just trying, whereas those who succeed do everything possible to make it happen and more. Those who fail at anything usually always say, "I tried," and those who succeed have an entirely different story of how committed they were and how they did everything possible to accomplish the goal. Be committed!

3. Accountability

Holding yourself accountable is the discipline behind goal setting. It is not good enough to just hold yourself accountable; you also need an accountability partner who holds you to a high standard. Most people have the wrong accountability partner because they are often let off the hook or just have someone they are sharing ideas with, but who is not holding their feet to the fire. The best accountability partner is one who clearly understands your goals and will make certain you accomplish them. He does not buy into your stories of why you can't or didn't do something. He is there to make sure you get it done—period, end of story! Make sure your accountability partner shares a mutual respect for the goals you're working on. It is also important to have an accountability partner who holds himself accountable for his goals.

4. Action Plan (Clear, Specific, and Strategic)

You've made the decision, you're 100 percent committed, and you're now accountable. The next step is an action plan. The challenge with a lot of people is that they have the wrong action plan. They are doing "things" that have little or nothing to do with the goal. They are throwing things against the wall hoping something will stick. You must create a plan that is clear, meaning you understand it fully. You must create a plan that is specific, meaning you know exactly what you must do and the order in which it must be done. You must create a plan that is strategic, meaning doing things the right way and at the right time. Thinking strategically will minimize mistakes, which will accelerate your progress. Having the ingredients doesn't mean anything if you do not have the correct recipe. The recipe will take you from where you are to where you want to go, and if it's done correctly, the result will appear every time. Remember that a goal without a plan is simply a wish. There must be a blueprint that is designed specifically for you, that is clear, specific, and strategic.

So you are now ready to create some goals for yourself. Remember, the question to ask is, "What if you cannot fail?" Also think of how you will feel once the goal is accomplished. Goals are like anything else. Once you accomplish one, the others are much easier. Condition yourself to be goal oriented, and you will always grow. Always challenge yourself and whenever you feel comfortable, do something differently. If you're not growing, you're dying. Goal setting coupled with the four steps mentioned and measuring your progress will keep you growing. Align yourself with people who support your goals. Tune out those who speak negatively. Look at your list of things you "should" do and convert them to things you "must and will do." Have fun and happy goal setting!

Basic Habits Of Successful People

There are behaviors and habits peculiar to the successful people in every country. In spite of the different climes they live in, it appears as if they live by a certain code of conduct known only to them and their families. In this section, I will deal with practical examples and how they can be applied to your lives.

Tom Corley, an accountant and financial planner, studied 233 wealthy individuals, most of whom were self-made millionaires. He compared his result to responses from 128 low-earning individuals. He then noticed that there are certain lifestyle choices that are to be cultivated if an individual has his eyes on success.

What are these behaviors and how do they affect the lives of these billionaires?

1. Getting Up Early

According to Corley, an astounding 50 percent of the billionaires interviewed admitted to waking up three hours before their workday actually started. Most of them use this free time to brainstorm new ideas, tackle personal problems, plan their day, read, or even exercise. This time of the day meets them fresh and still bright, so most activities they do end up being of high quality.

Benjamin Franklin once said, "Early to bed and early to rise makes a man healthy, wealthy, and wise." Most successful people have taken this advice to the extent Benjamin never thought of. The CEO of AOL told the *Guardian* that he wakes around 5:00 or 5:15 in the morning, either to reply to e-mails or work out. "Historically, I would start sending e-mails when I got up. But not everyone is on my time schedule, so I have tried to wait until 7 a.m. Before I e-mail, I work out, read and use our products," he told the *Guardian*.

The CEO of Disney, Robert Iger, wakes at 4:30 every morning, so he can enjoy a "little quiet time" to himself. In 2009, he told the *New York Times*, "It's a time I can recharge my batteries a bit. I exercise and clear my head, and I catch up on the world. I read papers. I look at e-mail(s). I surf the web. I watch a little TV, all at the same time."

Another successful personality who also rises before the sun is Tim Cook, the CEO of Apple. He is known for getting up and sending the company e-mails at 4:30 a.m., according to *Gawker*'s Ryan Tate. By 5:00 a.m., he is already in the gym, working out.

These billionaires do it, but what are the underlying benefits of rising early?

1. Mental fitness: One very important aspect of waking up early is reduced stress level. When you wake up early, it destroys the chances of you rushing in the morning, or forgetting vital materials. The day starts with a healthy dose of optimism, and such positivity is bound to stay with you throughout the day.
2. Better sleep quality: For you to rise early, you have to go the bed quite early. If sleeping early becomes an established routine in your life, it translates into a better sleep quality due to the fact that your body's internal clock adapts to the new system.
3. Better productivity: This is perhaps the most important reason for waking up early. This time of the day has proven to be the most productive time of the day for most individuals, including the successful ones. At this time of the day, there are no distractions. Waking

up early gives you a great opportunity to do what others will do when the day properly kicks off, hence giving you an edge over them. You could spend the time working out, replying to e-mails, brainstorming, completing a personal or work project, and so many other things.

4. Solitude: Tame Impala, a music group, has a song titled, "Solitude Is Bliss." The title of the song holds so much truth it becomes hard to ignore and easier to envision and wish for that solitude. The early-morning hours are usually so peaceful and quiet. It could be your private hour, reflecting on your mistakes and figuring out ways to stop them. You could also draw your plans at this period, because of the *bliss* it affords.

5. Breakfast: Yes! Breakfast. Many times, due to us rushing off to work, we often just take a slice of bread or an apple, and we rush straight to our car or the bus station and off to work. Waking up early affords you the chance to have one of the most important meals of the day.

6. Motivation: According to a research by the biologist Christoph Randler of Harvard University, early risers are more motivated. He conducted an experiment on proactivity, and the results showed that morning people are more proactive than night people. In the study, early risers accepted the fact that they spent more time setting long-term goals for themselves, and they felt confident and motivated.

We have studied the importance of waking up early, but how do we achieve that feat? It is easy if you follow these steps religiously:

1. Start slowly: Out of excitement and a need to feel the various benefits rising early has to offer, it is natural to feel the need to make drastic changes so as to achieve the required effect. It is advised to start slowly. You could set the alarm fifteen to thirty minutes earlier than usual. Do this for a few days, before reducing it by ten minutes. Then study your sleep for a few weeks and try to wake without the use of the alarm. Continue doing this until you get to your goal time.

2. Go to sleep earlier than normal: You might be used to staying up late watching a TV series, or surfing the Internet, or even working late into the night. But for you to become an early riser, you have to stop this habit. Go to bed earlier, even if you believe you won't sleep. You could pick a book and read while in bed. If you are really tired, you might fall asleep sooner than you expected.

3. Place your alarm clock far away from your bed: You might have heard of this, but that doesn't change the fact that it works! When you have your alarm right beside your bed, there's a chance you might shut it off as soon as it rings. But when you have to stand up from the bed to turn it off, you are up already. So instead of going back to the bed, walk to the bathroom and urinate or wash your face (whichever works for you). By the time you have done this, you are awake enough to face the day.

4. Have a candid reason: Why are you choosing to wake up earlier than usual? Is there a project you'd like to have completed in record time? Are you just interested in the benefits? Whatever your reason is, make sure it's something important enough to motivate you to get up every morning.

5. Make maximum use of that extra time: Don't wake up early and waste that precious time. Use it to do something you have been wanting to do. Make that time worthwhile.

2. Exercising

Even though, according to Tom Corley's research, not all the millionaires attested to exercising, 76 percent confirmed that exercising is a priority to them. They admitted that they spent thirty minutes or more doing aerobic exercise every day.

Richard Branson says that his morning routine of waking up by 5:00 a.m. to play tennis or to bike has doubled his productivity. In a recent blog, the serial entrepreneur says, "I seriously doubt that I would have been as successful in my career (and happy in my personal life) if I hadn't placed importance on my health and fitness."

Also, Mark Zuckerberg is one of the successful men who takes exercising to heart. He believes staying in shape is very important. He stresses that "doing anything well requires energy, and you just have a lot more energy when you are fit." Mark works out at least three times a day, and it is usually the first thing when he wakes.

The CEO of Twitter and Square, Jack Dorsey, reportedly has an eighteen-hour work day. He considers exercise his escape, a way to get more out of his already-packed schedule. In an AMA on *Project Hunt*, he revealed, "Up at 5:00, meditate for 30, seven-minute workout times three, make coffee, check in…"

Health: Working Out/Exercise

Basically, exercising means any form of body movement that involves the muscles and causes your body to lose calories. There is a range of physical activities including running, jogging, walking, jumping, dancing, and so many others. Being active, according to current and past research, has shown to confer a lot of health and psychological benefits.

Shall we explore some of its merits?

1. Happiness: Exercising has been proven to boost your mood and decrease feelings of anxiety, depression, and stress. It effects changes in the parts of the brain that regulate stress and anxiety. Also, it increases the brain's sensitivity to serotonin and norepinephrine, which relieves you of depression.

    In addition, exercise increases the production of endorphins, which help produce positive feelings and reduce the perception of pain. In conclusion, regular exercise can improve your mood and reduce feelings of anxiety and depression.

2. It is good for the muscles and bones: Exercise plays a significant role in building and maintaining the body's muscles and bones. Exercise helps

release hormones that promote the ability of your muscles to absorb amino acids. These acids, in turn, help the muscles grow and reduce the chance of a breakdown.

Younger people have an edge over their older counterparts. For young people, exercise builds bone density, which prevents osteoporosis when you are older.

3. Exercising will build your brain and help you break bad habits: Instead of crashing behind a TV with snacks in your hands after a hard day at work, choosing to exercise over these seemingly rewarding activities puts your mind in contact with your body, hence creating focus and a time to purge your mind of all worries and plans. It gives you the chance to collect your thoughts, instills a sense of direction in you, and prevents scenarios of indecision and indulgence.

Exercising helps break bad habits because it allows all pressures of responsibility to slide away with your dripping sweat, replacing those pressures with assurance and strength for the future.

4. Increased self-esteem: Working out reduces stress and also teaches that you can excel beyond the boundaries you have set for yourself. While building your body and mind into something smarter, it trains you to believe more in yourself. With the extra fifty meters you choose to run every morning, that habit would teach you to believe you can conquer new ground, to believe more in yourself and the great things you can achieve.

5. You will work smarter, not harder: According to the blog, *ENTREPRENEUR*,

> We know corporate retreats are a great way to increase morale and team build. Unfortunately, these tend to be harder to put together and happen infrequently. However, a pickup basketball game or company baseball game can be done fairly easily and can lead to similar results. Plus, unlike some retreats, they are a great and fun way to exercise and light the fire in your belly!

Having a regular commitment outside the office can be incredibly necessary. Just as you can burn out from overexercise, you can hit a point of diminishing returns if you stay much longer than eight hours at the office. Scheduled or spontaneous workout time can help you make the most of your work time by keeping you aware that when it's quitting time, it's really quitting time. And it is comforting to know that even if you're not at work, you're building a more focused, more productive you. Doing it with coworkers has the added benefit of bringing everyone together and maybe even solving a few problems on the court!

Remember, this advice is not about getting bikini-ready or becoming an Adonis. It's about getting in shape, inside and out, to tackle the most important challenges. It's about creating patterns in your life that bring about the best you possible. After all, the politicians and celebrities above aren't fictional characters. They're real people who have seen real results, and that can be you too! Give your body the attention it deserves, and your professional life will follow suit. If you want to build a strong career, you'll need the strength to build it.

Exercising: How? This Is For Starters

1. Start slow: This is just like the last section of waking up early. To efficiently master a habit, you have to start slowly, but steadily. This way, it becomes easy to increase your time commitment slowly. You can start by simply taking a ten-minute walk each day for a week. The next week, start running, or any exercise of your choice, but for about fifteen minutes this time.

2. Keep records of your progress: You could start a journal where you record your daily progress and the way you felt about it. Trust me, your comments for the day might be the reason you are willing to go on another run the next day.

3. Be kind to yourself: Do not start working out today and expect to start seeing the effects the next day. Don't beat yourself up when you fail to see any improvements, or when you fail to reach a mark. Look at your past mistakes and unhealthy choices as a chance to learn and grow.

4. Choose activities that make you happy: If the workout you do doesn't make you smile, there's a chance you wouldn't be willing to do it the next time. You don't have to run or visit the gym like everyone else. Do what fits your lifestyle, abilities, and taste. Is it swimming? Squatting? Go ahead!

5. Reward yourself: When you are starting an exercise program, it is good to give yourself immediate rewards. This way, you always look forward to it whenever the words "working out" cross your mind.

3. Read: Gaining more knowledge and insight can never harm you; this is a fact that most successful people have known and practiced for years. They have stocked their libraries, offices, and homes with books. Steven Siebold has interviewed 1,200 of the richest people in the world in the past thirty-one years. In his book, *How Rich People Think*, Steven says, "Walk into a rich person's home and one of the first things you'll see is an extensive library of books they've used to educate themselves on how to become more successful."

   It has been well publicized that the CEO of Hathaway, Warren Buffett, spends an astounding 80 percent of his time reading. His right-hand man, Charlie Munger, is also a bookworm. He reads so much his children think he's a "book with a couple of legs sticking out."

   Elon Musk, CEO of Tesla and SpaceX, attributes his brilliance and ideas to books. While growing up, he would read as many as two books per day. He says he reads for pleasure, but basically for knowledge.

Importance Of Reading

1. Reading activity leads to professional success: W. Fusselman proclaimed, "Today a reader, tomorrow a leader." And President Harry S. Truman told everyone, "Not all readers are leaders, but all leaders are readers."

   In 2017, Dr. Alan Zimmerman writes on CompTIA's blog,

   > From first-hand experience I know that is the truth. As a professional speaker, I've had the opportunity to speak in hundreds and hundreds of organizations. And I've worked directly with many of their top leaders, and they're always talking about what they're reading and what they're learning.
   >
   > Just this last week, I spoke at the all-company meeting for BeckAg, an incredibly innovative, tech-savvy, agricultural communication company. As I was eating dinner with Stephanie Liska, the President of BeckAg, she turned to me and asked what was the best book I've read recently and shared the books that had the biggest impact on her personal and professional lives.
   >
   > The experience was not an unusual one for me. Time after time, I've had Presidents, CEOs, CFOs, VPs, business owners

and the like talk to me about the books they're reading and the difference it's making. I know for a fact that leaders are readers.

The lesson seems to be inescapable. If you want to get ahead, be better, or have more, you need to be an active reader.

2. Reading opens up a world of opportunities: Walt Disney understood that there were more treasures in books than all the pirate's loot on Treasure Island. Books contain a horde of information, and one of them might just be what you are looking for. Read widely and enthusiastically. You have to understand that you have to read before the need arises.
3. Poor reading skills are a prerequisite for failure.

How To Develop Enviable Reading Skills

1. Read any material you come across.
2. Join book clubs.
3. Create a schedule for books you want to read or allocate a certain number of pages for a day. It could be fifty pages a day, or less; basically, whatever works for you.

Life Lessons

Everything won't be easy, smooth, and comfortable. Problems and dilemmas will arise, almost forcing you to give up. We can also learn from the mistakes of others—common mistakes.

I found this as my team and I were researching for stories of successful people. It was written by Britany Powell.

1. The first several jobs you take won't be interesting: "Come back when you have experience," they say. But how is one to gain experience if nobody will hire until one is already experienced? All successful people have had to take a job—or two, or three—that act only as stepping stones within a greater picture. They weren't fun, they weren't relevant, they weren't satisfying, but they get you where you want to go.
2. You will be told off time and time again: Communication is necessary in business. Some people may not be as sensitive in their going about it as your ego would like, but it is nothing personal, just business.
3. Life will not be easy: The road to success promises lots of hardship early on. Many will lose hope when the trials become too much to handle, but sticking it out is what makes the successful truly successful.
4. Your relationships will be tested: In times of choice, where a course of action must be taken, the relationships around you will prove to be

either supportive or detrimental to your success. Who is backing you up? And who couldn't care less?

5. Eat, sleep, breathe work: At one point or another, you will have to devote yourself fully to your goals. At this inflection point, every successful person has had to put themselves into high gear to make the final push toward a breakthrough.

6. Sometimes mistakes will cost you: Many people are forgiving of little mistakes; however, from time to time, there are mistakes that will cost you your position. It's a dreadful prospect to think of, but it's happened to the best of them.

7. Don't let the first big win go to your head: After all of the struggles, a major success is worth celebrating! Celebrate indeed, but don't let it cloud your vision of hard work.

8. Enjoy the journey: Life passes by all too quickly and oftentimes, the journey is the most exciting part. Don't wish for the end, when your dream is a reality, because then the story will be over. Enjoy the moment and take all that life puts before you in stride.

9. Family is important: Cherish your family. Others will come and go, but those you hold closest to your heart will be there for you in the best and the worst of times. You need not be surrounded by your flesh and blood; family does not have to be biological. Find those you call your family and stick together. Life is so much more special when surrounded by loved ones.

10. Remember who you are and where you came from: The road can be long and winding; lots of influences and voices coaxing you this way or that. It is up to you to decide what is right and what is best. Never forget, however, to look back every once in a while. Be proud of your beginnings and make sure you can be proud of what you are now.

Why Failure Is Important

On the *LifeHacker* blog, Katherine Eion had this to say:

1. Accept failure, but keep trying.

Michael Jordan once said that, "I can accept failure, everyone fails at something. But I can't accept not trying." Failure then becomes a means to an end, rather than an end in and of itself. In other words, failure is a part of the journey toward success. Everyone fails at one time or another, the courage part comes in continuing to try.

2. Continue forward in spite of failure. Keep trying.

Walt Disney was fired because he "lacked imagination and had no good ideas." Here is the man responsible for an empire of imaginative movies and play for children the world over, and yet, he lost his job due to a lack of imagination. The lesson here is to keep moving toward that end goal, even when other people fail to see the same vision.

3. Success or failure is dependent upon whether or not you keep at it.

Babe Ruth said that, "Every strike brings me closer to the next home run." This lesson is similar to Edison's remark about his light bulb. Like it or not failure is the very engine of success, moving us one step closer to a successful conclusion. Of course, this also means that you have to keep going and not quit in attempting to achieve your goal.

4. Sometimes failure simply means changing direction.

Love Ben and Jerry ice cream? So do I. Here were a couple of guys that had completely different directions for their lives and still managed to become admirably successful. Mr. Ben Cohen dropped out of college, while Mr. Jerry Greenfield failed to get into medical school, and both managed to become and remain wildly successful.

5. Believe in yourself.

Not everyone is going to "get you." Elvis was told to pack it in and go home due to his "astounding" lack of talent. Yet, can you imagine a world without his talent when he was at his peak and now he's a worldwide legend? Success begins through believing in what you can do. Don't let other people discourage you in your path toward success.

6. Failure is a chance to learn.

Henry Ford is quoted as saying, "Failure is simply the opportunity to begin again, this time more intelligently." Certainly, Edison would agree. You've just learned all the wrong ways toward that particular success, as Edison did with his "ten thousand" wrong attempts. Every lesson learned, every failure, is a movement in the right direction.

7. Attitude about failure can make all the difference.

"Success is the ability to go from failure to failure without losing your enthusiasm," said Sir Winston Churchill. England was at a great disadvantage with the advent of World War II. Here is a prime example of tiny David against mighty Goliath. Churchill's enthusiastic belief in England's defense was a part of the turning point for that country in the war.

8. Courage must be your watchword.

"If you have made mistakes, even serious ones, there is always another chance for you. What we call failure is not the falling down, but the staying down," a quote from Mary Pickford. We are all quite capable of spectacular mistakes and some of us, myself included, have made them. The key is to not allow defeat and failure to be the end-all. You must continue forward.

9. Don't give up.

"For every failure, there's an alternative course of action. You just have to find it. When you come to a road block, take a detour," a quote from Mary Kay Ash. She was the founder of the very successful home business for leading cosmetics. Perhaps, the lesson of the failure is that there may be a better or a different way to achieve your goal."

10. Success can only grow from failure.

Benjamin Disraeli, a former British Prime Minister said, "All my successes have been built on my failures." Indeed, failure is only a tipping point when one is on the road to success. Without failure, we as humans don't learn and our movement toward success is stagnated. Let failure guide you toward success instead of becoming the stopping point.

The one common thing all successful people have is a past of failures. If you are afraid to fail or unwilling to fail, you do not deserve to succeed. We learn far more from our failures than we ever will from our successes. It's important when you fail to fail forward, meaning do not repeat those same mistakes. One of the best ways to avoid failure is to align yourself with those who are success-fully doing what you aspire to do. You must also be coached by someone who has made those mistakes so that you don't have to repeat them. This is the value of coaching and why it is so important in everyone's life whether you are an entrepreneur or not. Failure is something that we all go through, and it makes us stronger and better. Minimizing the failure is the goal, and taking those lessons should motivate you to succeed. When you fail at reaching a goal, never change the goal; change the plan you were on that lead you to the failure. When you change your mind-set about failure and setbacks, you eliminate the fear that is associated with them.

Conclusion

This book is only a guide to success. The original and only path to success is in you. The only person who can stop you from being who you were meant to be is you. To be successful is simple: follow the rules, but bend them a little; follow your heart, but never let it get in the way of common sense.

Success involves trying and failing. Trying again. Maybe failing, but still trying. Thomas Edison said, "Our greatest weakness lies in giving up. The most certain way to succeed is always to try just one more time." Success is no accident. It is hard work, perseverance, learning, studying, sacrifice and most of all, love of what you are doing or learning to do.

I hope that the lessons in this short book have inspired you to take action to become the person you want to be. We all have the ability to succeed. We all have the potential to succeed. Success doesn't discriminate based on age, background, religion, color, or where you currently are economically. No matter your background or things you've done in the past, you too can succeed at whatever it is you want to do. Never let someone tell you otherwise. Align yourself with great people who believe in you and who hold you accountable to your goals, and never, ever slow down. I wish you much success in life and business, and I hope to meet you in person one day. Until then, may you have a life full of greatness and fulfillment.

Made in the USA
Columbia, SC
17 February 2024

31747026R00061